SPECTACULAR STORIES
FOR CURIOUS KIDS
SPORTS EDITION

Contents

The Last Second Shot That Was Truly Life or Death

There were just two seconds left in the game. His team was down by 3 points. This would take a miracle. And this was the quarterfinals of the SEC men's college basketball tournament. This was a big, BIG moment.

Mykal Riley of Alabama, sprints around his teammate who screens the Mississippi State defender, setting him free. He's 4 feet beyond the 3-point line and catches the ball. The clock has already dropped to 1.4 seconds. He jumps, drifting left, and flicks the ball toward the basket with 0.8 seconds left on the clock.

This is the moment that kids everywhere shooting hoops in the backyard always dream of. But this was no simple last-second shot. Little did Mykal know at the time, but if he misses...hundreds of people would probably die.

The shot goes in and the fans go crazy. Overtime! This game isn't over yet. And it's a good thing because 8 minutes after Mykal's miracle shot swished through the net, completely unknown to fans and players, a deadly killer passed right by the stadium. A huge EF2 tornado blew right by the Georgia Dome in downtown Atlanta, Georgia where the game was (fortunately) still being played.

The roof of the dome started to rumble. The scoreboards swayed. Security guards were running down the halls shouting for everyone to get away from the windows and doors. A hole was torn in the wall sending insulation falling to the court like snow.

The tornado was leaving nothing but destruction in its path. If Mykal's shot had missed, the game would have ended 8 minutes earlier, just the perfect amount of time for thousands of fans to have filed out of the building and been outside on the way to their cars. They would have been in the direct path of the tornado and its deadly mayhem. Glass from broken windows flew everywhere with cars being flipped over. Had people been out there, it would have been a disaster.

A tornado is a column of air that rotates violently extending from a thunderstorm cloud down to the ground. Tornadoes are rated on a scale based on their wind speeds and the amount of damage they cause.

The tornado that went through Atlanta on March 14, 2008, was an EF2 tornado. That meant it had wind speeds of 111-135 miles per hour and did considerable damage. It left a path of destruction through the city that was 6 miles long and 200 yards wide. The Georgia Dome took damage to its roof. Other notable buildings that were damaged were the CNN Center and the Georgia World Congress Center. One person died and thirty more were injured. It could have been so much worse though if all of those basketball fans would have been outside of the building.

And really, the Mississippi State fans would probably have still been jumping up and down celebrating the win watching their players hugging and joyful. The thousands of Alabama fans that were so happy when Mykal's shot went in, had no idea that not only had he kept Alabama alive in the game, but his shot was likely keeping them alive as well.

But how did Mykal make it to that basketball court in that exact moment on that exact team? There's a lot more to this story.

In 1994, in Pine Bluff, Arkansas, 9-year-old Mykal got an incredible gift. His grandmother had a full basketball court put in her backyard. It was a gorgeous rectangle of concrete, hoops, 3-point lines, foul lines, and surrounded by chicken wire to keep the ball from getting out into traffic. She even had floodlights installed. She wasn't a wealthy woman, but she was very dedicated to her grandchildren and her community.

Over the next few years, young Mykal spends thousands of hours on that court. But in high school, he's not as big as the kids on the team. Luckily, the coach lets him be the team manager or water boy. Mykal is shy but works hard. And he finally makes the varsity team in 12th grade. He's not a starter and is nervous to actually shoot. He's not very good at defense either. The team wins a championship that year but Mykal only gets on the court for about 5 minutes in that final game.

Shockingly, just two months after the end of the basketball season, Mykal grows 4 inches taller! His high school coach can't believe it and calls a friend who coaches at a small college in Arkadelphia, Arkansas who gets Mykal on his team that fall.

Mykal struggles with grades and drops out of college. He never played one minute for that basketball team. He goes back home and starts going to a small college back in Pine Bluff but doesn't last long there either. But he keeps playing and shooting in his grandmother's backyard and grows *another* 2 inches. He's now 6 foot 6 inches tall!

Mykal's high school coach happens to run into another small college basketball coach at a basketball game and tells him about Mykal. That coach, from Panola College in Carthage, Texas, drives the 4 hours to see Mykal play in the gym and offers him a scholarship. Finally, Mykal plays college basketball... and flourishes. Panola runs the perfect system for him and he averages 16 points per game. Bigger colleges start to notice.

The coach of the University of Alabama flies in to see him and brings him on that team which was big-time basketball. Mykal continues to get better and better. When he was a college senior, Alabama had its worst season in 10 years and limped into the year-end conference tournament. But...their first game is against the defending champion of the last two years in a row, Florida. Alabama is not even supposed to make it a close game. But Mykal scores 26 points and they pull off the big upset.

Next, they have to play the best team in the tournament, Mississippi State. It's a tough game and by the end of it, Mykal is exhausted. It all comes down to one play. And this kid who had survived the tough streets of Pine Bluff, who had to be a water boy and barely played in high school, had dropped out of 2 colleges, this determined kid who had worked SO hard for so many years, finally found his moment to be a star. And Mykal Riley was more than that, he became a hero. And he did that by never giving up on himself.

But I haven't told you who won the game! With one second left in overtime, Mykal once again had a chance to tie the game and send it to a 2nd overtime. But his shot rimmed around the hoop and fell out giving Mississippi State the win. That was the last shot Mykal took for Alabama. But by that time, the danger had already passed. Mykal never regretted it and is happy for his place in history. And even though he never played in the NBA, Mykal enjoyed a long, successful career playing professional basketball in Europe.

The Shocking Historical Figure in the Wrestling Hall of Fame

You're about to learn something completely crazy. I had no idea myself. There was once a guy in the western part of the Illinois frontier in the early 1800s who wrestled around 300 people and only lost once. You know all about him. Well, not everything, obviously. You've been studying him in school since you were little. You just don't know about this part of his life.

A small crowd had gathered around to watch the match. It was over in a flash. The tall and lanky victor had won with just one toss of his opponent and yelled loudly at the crowd around him. "I'm the big buck of this lick. If any of you want to try it, come on and whet your horns!" Nobody made a peep as he stalked about eyeing them with a face full of rage and menace. So who am I talking about? Any guesses?

This was before he became our 16th president...I'm talking about a young Abraham Lincoln. Surprised? This probably doesn't quite match the image of him that you've always gotten from your school textbooks. We tend to think of Abraham Lincoln as a soft-spoken, mild-mannered bookworm beanpole with a beard and top hat. And he was all of those things. But he was also an incredibly accomplished fighter when he was young.

One story is particularly fun. In Abraham's hometown of New Salem, Illinois, he worked at the general store. And this town had a bully. His name was Jack Armstrong. Jack was the leader of a gang of rascals that would play dirty tricks on new people who came to town. This gang was known as the Clary's Grove Boys. Their favorite pastime was putting a person in a barrel and nailing it shut. Then they would laugh hysterically as they rolled the poor guy in the barrel down a steep hill. The people of New Salem knew that their best bet was that tall Abraham kid over at the general store. Jack was fed up hearing about how he had never put Abraham in a barrel and only picked on people that he could beat up. So he challenged Abraham to duel, a wrestling duel.

All the Clary's Grove Boys were there. The whole town showed up on the big day. Abraham, our future president, had already won around 300 wrestling matches by this point. This would be a tough match, even for a bully like Jack. In this particular match, you won by throwing your opponent, not by pinning them on the ground. There are multiple accounts of this match but the following seems to be the most credible. The two men circled one another and then the grappling began. They were both strong. Neither could get the better of the other at first. As they kept at it, Jack began to get worn out by Abraham. Jack was getting desperate and went to trip Abraham which was considered cheating. It wasn't a good idea to use dirty tricks against "Honest Abe". That only made him mad, really mad.

Abraham grabbed Jack's neck and according to witnesses, "shook him like a rag." That was when all the Clary's Grove Boys moved in, pinning Abraham to the wall of the general store. This didn't sit well with our hero either. He told them that he'd fight every last one of them in a fair one-on-one fight. That was when Jack called off the fight and his gang. Abraham had won and everyone knew it, even Jack. Jack called Abraham "the best 'feller' that ever broke into this settlement," and the two men shook hands. Abraham was still undefeated. But now he was a local hero for beating the town bully.

When Abraham started campaigning to become president, his career as a wrestler came up and eventually helped him as people saw it as a good leadership quality. He spoke about it during one of his political campaigns when he talked about his one and only defeat as a wrestler. It was during a military conflict known as the Black Hawk War. It was a war between the United States armed forces and the Sauk Native American people whose leader was named Black Hawk. Lincoln served in the army during that war and during some downtime, the men would have wrestling matches to see who was the toughest. Abraham fought a man named Hank Thompson. It was a fierce fight, but Abraham was thrown twice and said when he lost, "Why, gentlemen, that man could throw a grizzly bear."

Abraham shared that story in 1860 with a professor whose father fought with Lincoln in that war. That would be the same year that he finally won the presidency. Abraham's reputation as a 6-foot 4-inch tall fighter with incredible strength during his 20s was legendary. And if he really only lost once in hundreds of matches, then he deserved that reputation. Historians seem to be in full agreement that his fighting career was completely factual. It's a little-known tidbit about our 16th president but he fought for around 12 years as a young man so it was a key part of his life. When you fight as a wrestler you have to be both tough and smart. You have to recognize your opponent's weaknesses. This probably helped Abraham during his political life and as a wartime president during the Civil War. It was in 1992 that the National Wrestling Hall of Fame inducted him officially as an "Outstanding American" in regards to wrestling. We all know that Abraham Lincoln was an outstanding American and one of our greatest presidents, but now you know just how tough he was and what a great athlete he was as well.

Case of the Stolen Bat, Mission Impossible Style

This story is hard to believe. Buckle up, it's a wild one. Fake ceilings, blatant cheating, thieves in ceilings, a pitcher with a missing toe...it's got it all.

In 1994, Albert Belle of the Cleveland Indians was on a tear. He was smashing home runs all over the place and the Indians were playing well. The thing was, Albert was cheating and the team knew it. His bat was corked. This meant that the bat had been hollowed out and the wood on the inside of the bat had been replaced with cork which is lighter. This allows a hitter to swing the bat faster which gives them more power. It's against the rules of baseball. It can be hard to catch since it's on the inside of the bat and can only be seen if you take a saw and cut through the bat or X-ray it.

Throughout baseball history, players have cheated in all kinds of ways. The corked bat has been one popular strategy. But it results in suspensions and it's really embarrassing to be caught cheating this way. Sometimes players are caught in funny ways like when they hit a ball and the bat breaks open. Uh oh! The cork flies out and it's pretty hard to miss. The player is ejected on the spot. "I don't know HOW that cork got in there!" "That's not my bat!" There are a lot of possible excuses.

The Indians were in Chicago playing the White Sox. Both teams were in the same division and battling for a playoff spot. Chicago's manager had somehow been tipped that Albert's bat was illegal so he challenged it. This meant that the umpire had to take the bat and check it after the game to see if it really was illegal. So the bat was taken to the umpires' dressing room and locked inside. Here's where the fun begins.

The players in the Indian dugout were not feeling good about this. They all knew that Albert's bats were corked. One pitcher who wasn't playing that day was Jason Grimsley. Jason had been in the major leagues for 5 years and this was his first season with the Indians. Jason was a bit of a rascal. Maybe that's why such a funny thought popped into his head as he was sitting there while all of this drama was unfolding. "Maybe I can get that bat!" That's a pretty good teammate. But it's also the kind of thought that could get you in a lot of trouble. Not only was Jason an adventurous rascal, but he was also observant. He noticed that the ceilings in the clubhouse were ceiling tiles that you could take out. So he figured that the umpires' room where Albert's bat had been locked away, had the same kind of ceiling.

Even though Jason was really tall at 6 feet and 3 inches, he thought he could climb through the air ducts into that umpires' room and steal the illegal bat for his teammate. Jason had grown up as a really active kid who loved jumping his dirt bike and climbing trees. Once, he hit a stump with his dirt bike as a

12-year-old and lost his big toe. Ouch! Okay, so he's an adventurous guy, but would he really fit in the ceiling? This was one supremely crazy idea. He calmly walked down the hallway where the locked umpires' room was and calculated how far it was from the visiting team's clubhouse. He thought it looked to be about 100 feet. He got another bat and was able to find a flashlight. Was he really going to do this?

He went into an office and climbed up onto the desk. He took out a ceiling tile and peeked up there shining the flashlight. It was just as he thought. The walls were made of cinder blocks, so if he crawled along the tops of the walls which were a little over a foot wide, he might be able to pull this off. If he fell over though, he would crash through someone's ceiling! Undeterred, Jason hoisted himself up into the ceiling and began his top-secret mission. It was dark up there and really, really hot. This would not be easy. There were water pipes everywhere, too. If he put his weight on them, they might burst open making a real mess. After about 40 minutes of sneaking along on his stomach above the ceiling without hardly any headroom and the flashlight in his mouth, Jason had made it to where he *thought* the umpires' room might be. He couldn't know for sure, he just had to guess.

He slowly and carefully lifted a ceiling tile. Oops! Wrong room. And even worse, there was a groundskeeper sitting down there! Jason would later say that the groundskeeper must have seen one of the ceiling tiles get lifted up and a pair of eyes peeking down at him. What would you have done if you saw that? Jason didn't move a muscle after setting the ceiling tile back down in place. He didn't hear anybody yelling, maybe he would be okay. After what seemed like forever, he moved over a few feet and tried what must be another room. Would this be the right one?

It was the umpires' room. He had guessed correctly. And even better, the room was empty. But how long would it remain empty? With his heart racing, Jason went for it. He climbed down onto the top of a refrigerator and then hopped all the way down to the ground. He knew he had to be quick. He saw Albert's bat in the umpires' locker and grabbed it. In its place, he put the other bat that he had dragged along. He climbed back up on top of the refrigerator and into the ceiling. As soon as he put the ceiling tile back in place, someone came into the room. That was TOO close! This really was like a spy movie. He couldn't risk the person hearing him move around in the ceiling so he had to wait until whoever it was left the room again.

After he heard them leave and the door closed, he started making his way back. Four innings had passed in the ball game by the time he made it back. He proudly told his teammates that he had done it. Mission success! They couldn't believe it. They all congratulated him as if he had won the game. Maybe Albert wouldn't be suspended after all. Cleveland even won the game, 3 to 2. But they couldn't relax quite yet. Now it was time for the bat inspection. The only reason that you're reading this and that I know about this story is that it didn't go very well for Jason or Albert from this point in the story. The umpires knew that *somehow,* someone had switched the bat. This was not the bat they had locked in the room. For one thing, the first bat had Albert's name on it. This bat didn't seem as shiny and was marked as belonging to first baseman, Paul Sorrento. Oops. Maybe Jason hadn't quite thought this caper all the way through. But in his defense, he later admitted that he couldn't have replaced the bat with another of Albert's bats because Albert didn't have ANY bats that weren't corked! The umpires also noticed that there were little clumps of ceiling tile on the floor. Then they looked up and saw some bent metal brackets near the ceiling that looked odd.

The White Sox organization was furious. The thought for sure that the Indians were cheating and now this? They wanted somebody to go to jail. The police were called and Major League Baseball flew in a former FBI investigator to get to the bottom of this strange incident. The investigator dusted the entire room for fingerprints and discovered how the thief had made it into the room. Now that everyone knew that the original bat had definitely been stolen, the Cleveland Indians were in *serious* trouble. They were threatened with a full-blown FBI investigation. But the league settled for the original bat being turned over. They sawed into it in front of Albert and Cleveland's general manager. Albert was busted and suspended. But Jason wasn't. Somehow he hadn't left any fingerprints behind and none of his teammates told on him. Only years later would he confess that he was the thief in this crazy story. At that point, everyone had a good laugh about it. But the White Sox probably didn't find it so funny. Right after he confessed, he went on to help the New York Yankees win two World Series. So for Jason, it all worked out in the end, but I don't recommend trying this at home!

The Biggest Loser in the History of Racing

What if I told you that there was once a horse that lost 113 races? How many do you think they won? 500? 1000? What if this horse never won a single race? How could a horse like that keep racing? And who could possibly care? I'll bet you have questions, too. This is the remarkable story of Haru Urara.

Haru Urara was a horse in Japan. Her name translates to "Beauty of Spring" or "Glorious Spring." She was bred to sell. Her owners would breed horses and then sell them to people who would race them. But nobody bought Haru Urara. So the owners, Nobata Farm, hired a trainer. His name was Dai Muneishi and he worked in Kochi. Kochi was one of the cheapest racetracks in the entire country to race a horse. That's because it was a local track that didn't do much business. Dai, stitched Hello Kitty faces onto Haru Urara's pink facemask and named her.

The Japanese people love horse racing. People all around the world love it. In most horse racing movies, the horse always wins in the end. As you know, this isn't that kind of story. Haru Urara began racing in 1998. In her first race, she came in last place. Of course. This race happened at the Kochi Racetrack in the city of Kochi. Kochi is in the south of Japan on the island of Tokushima. There's not much close to it. It's remote.

The late '90s and early 2000s were a really tough time in Japan. The stock market had crashed. The economy was doing terribly. It was hard for people to find jobs. A little remote city like Kochi did not do well at all during a time like this. It was really hard on everyone all over the country. It was hard on the Kochi Racetrack too. People didn't have much money to place bets on horses. The people who worked at the track were trying to come up with clever ways to get customers. All the businesses in Kochi were trying hard to get customers. They had to if they wanted to survive.

Most horses, if they lose a few races or don't show much promise, are retired. Or worse, they are killed. But Haru Urara kept racing. And she kept losing. But she was really cute. She would practically prance into the starting gates for every race as if she thought that this time, maybe this time...she would win. She was a plucky, spirited mare. She did *not* like to train. She didn't like baths either. She would kick and stomp and try to run away. But in each race, she ran as hard as she could. People said that she would even seem to pose for pictures if someone took out a camera. By now the Kochi racetrack was in big trouble. They would have to close if they kept losing money. So they contacted their local newspaper and told them about their cute horse who could never win. The reporter thought it sounded interesting and wrote a story about the horse that had lost more than 80 races at this point. The story got picked up by bigger newspapers. Then even TV news stations heard about the horse. Soon, everyone all over the country knew about the cute loser horse all the way down in the little town of Kochi. People started writing fan letters and going to her races.

With everyone feeling depressed because life had been so hard for so long, there was something really cheerful about a horse that kept trying to win. It made people feel like they could keep going too, even though life was hard. As Hara Urara kept racing (and kept losing), she became the talk of the country. She had a beautiful name and she was so cute and brave. People started selling t-shirts and little stuffed horse toys that looked like her. She became more and more popular with every loss. This might be one of the only times in sports history where that has happened. Most people (and horses) give up when things don't go well. That's what was so heartwarming and amazing about Haru Urara. She kept going. People would place bets that she would win and those tickets became good luck tokens even though she kept losing.

After Haru Urara had lost a staggering 105 races is when the big event took place. The best jockey in all of Japan would ride her to try to get her a win. The excitement across the country was electric. The jockey was Yutaka Take and he had won more than 3,000 horse races. He was a celebrity. He was more than that. He was a horse racing legend. This was Haru Urara's big moment, this was her chance! On the day of the race, there were 3,000 people there before the Kochi Racetrack had even opened. People waited in line for 5 hours. There would be more than 13,000 people at the track to watch this race. Kochi Racetrack had *never* had anywhere near this many people show up before. It was a party. The day started as a rainy one and the track was muddy. Just as their hero came out, the clouds parted and the sun shone through for the first time that day. Everyone took it as a sign. This would truly be the thing they had all been waiting for. It could only mean that their hero was about to win her first race after 105 attempts. The massive crowd (and all of Japan) held their breath as their beloved, cute loser walked into the starting gate.

Then the bell sounded. They were off! Haru Urara didn't get the best start but that was okay. Surely she would catch up. 12 horses ran quickly around the first turn. The crowd gasped. Shoulders slumped. Haru Urara was trying, but even with the legendary Yutaka on her back, she just could not run fast. She fell far behind. She would finish in next to last place, nowhere near the winner. There were tears in the crowd. There was sadness. But then something really special happened. The other horses moved off the track after the race. Yutaka was behind them, but he stopped. The crowd started to yell thank you's to Haru Urara. They still loved her. These fans had bet nearly $1 million dollars that Haru Urara would win. But she did what she always did. A horse that had lost 105 times wasn't going to start winning now no matter who was riding her. But oddly, that didn't matter. She had given them something more valuable than money. Haru Urara had given them hope.

As Yutaka sat there on her back listening to the crowd yell that they loved her, he was moved. This was like nothing he had ever experienced in a losing race before. But none of this was like anything that *anybody* had ever experienced before. Yutaka could tell that the crowd wanted more. Amazingly, he took Haru Urara, the cute little horse who had inspired millions of people when they really needed it, on a...***victory lap***? This is probably the only time in the history of horse racing that a horse that finished in 11th place would do something like this.

The crowd went absolutely bonkers when they saw what Yutaka was doing. They yelled and they screamed. They cried. They put their arms around each other and laughed and cheered. Yutaka and Haru Urara slowly trotted around to track to the deafening roar of 13,000 fans. It was a magical moment. Nobody cared at all that she had not won. None of that mattered. This was the little horse who tried and kept on trying. And by doing that, she gave an entire nation the strength to do that too.

With all the money that people had bet on Haru Urara, the Kochi Racetrack was saved, and you can still watch horse racing there today. After a few more races, Haru Urara would finally retire after 113 losses and zero wins. She would live a happy life on a nice farm. She was still a famous celebrity and her face was used on posters asking people to drive safely. The police officers sent her over 1300 pounds of carrots as a thank you. Sometimes, things work out even if you don't win. That should give hope to all of us.

That Time a Soccer Team Stopped a War

Soccer (or football as it's known in most of the world) is a really big deal. It's the world's most popular sport. And when countries play against each other, national pride is on the line. All of this leads up to one of sport's biggest events every four years, the World Cup. This is the international soccer tournament that decides which country is the best in the world.

There's a huge amount of pressure on the teams that are expected to do well. But at every World Cup tournament, there are countries who are there for the first time that are simply thrilled to be there. For instance, at the 2018 World Cup, the Central American nation of Panama qualified for the very first time. Their first game was a 3-0 loss to Belgium. And in their next game against England, they were losing 6-0. That's a really lopsided score in soccer. But Panama then scored to make it 6-1. This was the country's first World Cup goal. It didn't matter that it meant a 6-point loss changed to a 5-point loss. The country went completely nuts celebrating their first-ever goal at this tournament. That's what a big deal the World Cup is.

Back in 2005, there was another national team that was hoping to qualify for the very first time. I'm talking

about the west African nation of the Ivory Coast. They had never been to a World Cup either. For a team to qualify for this international tournament, they have to win a bunch of qualifying games to earn a place. There was only one qualifying game left for the Ivory Coast team that year and they were behind the African soccer powerhouse of Cameroon, who had competed in the World Cup 5 times. Ivory Coast had to beat Sudan. But they also needed help. They needed Egypt to beat Cameroon. The two games would be played at the same time, 1600 miles apart, and would decide which country went to the World Cup and which would stay home.

The Ivory Coast played great. Sudan wasn't that good that year and they won the game 3-1. Then the players all piled into their locker room to await their fate. Would they make it? C'mon Egypt, please!

Cameroon was tied 1-1 with Egypt. The Ivory Coast players were thrilled! If the game ended in a tie, they would make history and their country would be represented in the World Cup for the very first time. The mood in the locker room was intense. It was nerve-racking to listen to the radio and hope that each time Cameroon got the ball that Egypt would somehow stop them from scoring. Then disaster struck. In the final seconds of the game, the referee awarded Cameroon a penalty kick, just one guy and the goalie. The Ivory Coast players were heartbroken. They were so close. Cameroon's players were really good. They didn't miss too many penalty kicks. Most penalty kicks ended up as goals no matter who was taking them. The goalie would have to guess which direction the player was kicking the ball and get lucky. The Ivory Coast needed a miracle.

People were also glued to their radios all over Cameroon. Pierre Wome, one of the best players in Cameroon soccer history, would take the kick. If he somehow missed, it meant that their team wouldn't make it to their 6th World Cup. The radio announcers were calling the shot. "Pierre is ready. He lines up, takes the kick, and...IT HIT THE POST! NO GOOD!"

He had missed. The Cameroon players couldn't believe it. They were devastated. Meanwhile, imagine the scene in Ivory Coast's locker room and all over the country! It was pandemonium. Pure joy. They had done it. But this is only part of the story.

What I haven't told you is that this was a terrible time for Ivory Coast. They had been in a deadly civil war for several years by the time this game was played. Rebel forces controlled the north. The south was under the control of an elected government. The first two years of the conflict were especially violent and deadly. But a buffer zone had been established and Ivory Coast was a country split in two. It was a very scary time in the history of the country.

But when the national soccer team qualified for the World Cup, both sides rejoiced. Suddenly, everyone felt a kinship that tied them together. The team itself was made up of players from all over the country, both the north and south. The Celebrations of the team's qualifying lasted all night long all over the country. For the first time in a long time, they all felt like they belonged to the same country. They were all Ivorians again rooting for the same team, the team that represented all of them.

Something truly special happened in that locker room after they knew they were bound for the World Cup. Their best player was Didier Drogba. He always led a prayer after every game. But after this game, a television crew had come into the locker room to record players' reactions. The players all stood arm in arm surrounding Didier who held a microphone. He addressed his nation.

"Men and women of Ivory Coast, from the north, south, center, and west, we proved today that all Ivorians can coexist and play together with a shared aim, to qualify for the World Cup. We promised you that the celebrations would unite the people. Today, we beg you on our knees." And with that, all the players around him got down onto their knees and Didier continued. "Forgive. Forgive. Forgive! The one country in Africa with so many riches must not descend into war. Please lay down your weapons. Hold elections. All will be better." Then with a smile on his face, Didier said, "We want to have fun, so stop firing your guns..." At that, the speech ends with the players back on their feet and singing that last line over and over.

This one-minute video clip was seen by everyone. It was powerful. It was moving. Everyone was reminded of what it felt like to be full of pride for their country.

Things began to change, slowly at first. The two entrenched sides that were bitter enemies began negotiating and finally, a ceasefire was agreed upon. The Ivory Coast team went on to the World Cup and played admirably, even winning two games against Serbia and Montenegro. They didn't make it out of the first round, but they had done their country proud and performed well by getting two victories.

A year later, Didier made a remarkable announcement. The Ivory Coast game against Madagascar would be played in the rebel capital of Bouake. This was a really big deal. It was an acknowledgment that people in the north mattered too. They would get to see their beloved team play. Didier was the most popular person in the country. He was from the south, but he was a man of peace. He was a leader.

The game was a massive event. It was basically a national holiday. But would the team win? It seemed to be their destiny. They scored again, and again and again. They were up 4-0 and everyone was celebrating wildly. But in the game's final minutes, a fairy tale ending presented itself. A ball was lofted near Madagascar's goal. Didier Drogba himself raced to it and skillfully dodged the goalie. He put the final stamp on the game by burying the ball in the back of the net for the final goal of the day. The noise that erupted from joyful fans was like a bomb going off. But this time it was a happy bomb. Many had traveled to Bouake for the first time in five years since the war had started. North and south celebrated together as one that day.

At that moment, it once again didn't matter what side of the country you were from. Fans rushed down to the field and enjoyed an amazing moment in history, united as Ivorians together. There would be no violence in Ivory Coast for several years. There was finally peace. Unfortunately, five years after this game, there would once again be fighting. To this day, Ivory Coast is still a country that is mostly divided. But for several years, a special team of soccer players brought peace and helped to end a war in their country.

Up Close & Personal with the Super Bowl Champs

Every Super Bowl is full of amazing stories. But this story is from Super Bowl 13 in 1979. It was a matchup of the mighty Dallas Cowboys who were the defending Super Bowl champs from 1978...and the stacked Pittsburgh Steelers who had won back-to-back Super Bowls just a couple of years earlier. The great Roger Staubach quarterbacked the Cowboys with the legendary Terry Bradshaw leading the Steelers. Both men had already won two Super Bowls. Only one would win their third in 1979.

But this game wasn't just about the quarterbacks. There were *twenty-five* future Hall of Famers playing in this game! Both teams were loaded with talent. The Steelers were winning 35-17 with just 7 minutes left in the game. Many were already celebrating on the sidelines. But the Cowboys were determined. Roger Staubach and his incredible running back, Tony Dorsett, kept making plays. And then Staubach found his tight end, Billy Joe Dupree, in the back of the endzone. TOUCHDOWN! Then the Cowboys amazingly recovered an onside kick to get the ball back. The celebrations stopped on the Pittsburgh sideline. Could the Cowboys pull this off? They scored yet another touchdown, getting to within 3 points.

The Steeler lead was now 35-31. The problem for the Cowboys was that there were just 22 seconds left in the game. They would have to get *another* onside kick.

Nobody in the stadium breathed as the Cowboys kicker lined up and put his hand in the air. It would all come down to this. After the play, Steeler fans erupted in the full euphoria that comes with seeing your team win a Super Bowl. Rocky Blier, one of Pittsburgh's running backs, had fallen on the ball. The game was over. The Steelers had won. But our story is just getting started. What would happen next in the Pittsburgh locker room would go down in football history as one of the wackiest, most daring acts by a football fan... ever.

Let me introduce you to the amazing Rick Steigerwald, a former golden gloves champion boxer, who was working as a pipefitter in Pittsburgh. Born and bred in Pittsburgh, Rick LOVED his home team, the Steelers. He had actually snuck into every home game that season. The Super Bowl was held down in Miami. So Rick, his brother, and some other friends made the long journey down to Miami and planned on sneaking into the game somehow.

Rick put a grappling hook in a black bag and hid it in the bushes the day before the game. Police officers made their patrols around the stadium on horseback and he timed them to know how long he would have to climb the fence. On the big day, he and his brother were standing there planning their move when suddenly a big group of people ran up and started hoisting themselves up the wall of the stadium after a patrol had passed by. Rick looked at his brother wide-eyed and ran to join them, leaving his grappling hook behind.

They and many others made it up to the roof where there was still a 12-foot fence to get over. They had drawn the attention of the police by this point who were yelling at them to come back down. They scaled the fence and with a little help from fellow Steeler fans, were in the stadium! They exchanged hugs with everyone who had made it and sauntered down to find some seats. Rick's luck wouldn't run out just yet. They went down near the 50-yard line in the center of the stadium and sat down. They were sitting near celebrities and famous football coaches and their families! They were all enjoying themselves during the pregame ceremony. Rick kept thinking, "What are we going to do when whoever has tickets for these seats show up?" Eventually, a man walked over and asked them if they had tickets as the game was ready to begin. This was bound to happen. Rick asked "Who are you? The ticket taker?" "No, no!" said the man. "My company bought this whole row of seats and nobody else showed up. You're welcome to sit there." Rick and his brother couldn't believe it. They hugged the nice guy and had the time of their lives watching their first live Super Bowl from some of the best seats in the stadium.

As the game was winding down, they thought, "Let's go get the game ball!" The Steigerwald brothers were definitely a pair of fun-loving rascals. They made their way down to the sideline and Rick was able to slip past the security guards. They stopped his brother but he kept moving quickly. He was dressed like the ball boys in sweatpants and a Steelers t-shirt. As the final seconds ticked off the clock, the Pittsburgh sideline swarmed the field. And there was Rick, right in the middle of all of it. Overjoyed and standing in the middle of the field, this was the moment of a lifetime for any Steeler fan.

Eventually, the team started to make their way to the locker room. So Rick, of course, jogged his way to where everyone else was going. Security stopped all the non-players and announced that the media would have to wait for a few minutes while the team got settled. Rick had found himself in a swarm of reporters and cameramen. He grabbed the cord of the cameraman in front of him and held it over his shoulder as if he was helping and walked into the locker room with the media members.

As soon as he was in there, he saw the game's MVP, Terry Bradshaw, standing at the podium waiting to be interviewed. Rick walked right up to him and told him what an incredible game it was. A confused Terry Bradshaw thanked him as they shook hands. Rick then saw a player that he had met before, Jack Deloplaine. Jack was confused to see Rick in the locker room but thought it was funny. Rick sat down next to him and explained how he had gotten in there. Suddenly a pack of reporters swarmed him saying

"Rick, Rick, Rick, can you give us an interview?" Rick looked at Jack confused.

Jack whispered to him that he was sitting at Rick Moser's locker! Both Rick Moser and Jack were Steeler running backs. So Rick Steigerwald kept playing along and answering questions about the game as if he was Rick Moser. Keep in mind that Rick Steigerwald is just five foot 6 inches tall and maybe the size of one of Rick Moser's legs. But the two men did both have mustaches at the time.

The reporters' questions went on for several minutes until one reporter said, "Rick, we don't want to hold you up. I'm sure you want to take a shower. Can we finish the interview after you've showered?" Rick hadn't thought of taking a shower! But it sounded like a good idea. Why not? "Sure, we can finish up fellas, after my shower," Rick told them. Jack Deloplaine just sat there completely bemused by what was happening.

Rick threw his clothes over Rick Moser's locker and sauntered into the showers. He found himself next to L.C. Greenwood, the six-foot 8-inch tall Steeler defensive end. L.C. looked down at him like "who's this guy?" Thinking quickly, Rick said "Hey man! I'm Chuck Noll's nephew, great game!" Chuck Noll was the Pittsburgh head coach. "Oh, hey man, how's it goin'?" L.C. asked him. Then he enthusiastically chatted with all the guys in the showers who thought he was related to their coach.

Then he gets a towel and heads back to the locker where the real Rick Moser sees him and just laughs as the imposter Rick once again gets swarmed by reporters. As he's finishing the interviews he sees a very unhappy player out of the corner of his eye who yells "Who is THAT!?!?!" looking at Rick. Rick is still naked with just a towel on and really tries hard to finish up the interviews as he realizes that he's busted. The player calls over the equipment manager who calls over security. The equipment manager is angry and the reporters all fade into the crowd, perhaps realizing they've been tricked. The security guards are huge football players themselves. They play for the University of Miami. The equipment manager wants Rick to be thrown out in nothing but his towel! But the two guards think the whole thing is really funny and let Rick get dressed. The good-natured guards walk him out, give him high fives, and leave Rick standing outside the locker room.

What an adventure! Rick turns to leave but sees hundreds of people lined up asking him for his autograph. He did just walk out of the players' locker room after all. So what else was he supposed to do? He gives out hundreds of autographs signing everything as his real name, Rick Steigerwald. Once he's done with the line of autograph seekers, he finds himself at the team bus. The driver also assumes he's a player (why else would people want his autograph?) and opens the door for him. The players aren't quite sure who he is though and all start to stare. Rick then makes a little speech about how amazing they all played and how proud of them he is. "Great game, guys!" he tells them as he turns back around and walks off the bus.

The way Rick's night went, it's actually surprising that he didn't just ride all the way back to the team hotel with his new friends. But he found his brother in the parking lot. His brother didn't believe a word of his story even after smelling the shampoo in his recently cleaned hair. That's the remarkable story of how Rick Steigerwald became a legend among fans of the Pittsburgh Steelers.

Baseball Player Turned Spy
With Orders to Kill

This is a doozy of a story and it's about a guy who might be one of the smartest people to ever play professional baseball. Even though he had an exciting sporting career, that might be one of the most boring things about him.

Moe Berg showed a lot of talent for both baseball AND sneakiness as a kid. If there was ever anyone who was destined to grow up to be both a baseball player AND a spy...Moe was that kid. Born Morris Berg, in 1902, everyone called him Moe. He grew up playing baseball in the streets of Newark, New Jersey. He showed a lot of brilliance as a student in his early years as well. Moe's family was Jewish and there weren't many Jewish kids at the school that he attended. When he joined a church baseball team who was looking for someone to play shortstop, he said his name was Runt Wolfe. What a hilarious fake name! Moe (I mean Runt) found that he really liked living a double life.

He graduated at the top of his class from a top college, Princeton, having studied and mastered lots and lots of languages. He studied Sanskrit and Latin and spoke German, French, Spanish, Greek, and Italian. Moe was extremely smart! His teammates always went to him for help with their classes. He and the 2nd baseman would speak in Latin on the field so the other team wouldn't know what they were saying.

When he graduated, Princeton offered him a job as a teacher but he decided to stick with baseball. He joined the Brooklyn Robins, who later became the Dodgers. In the offseason, he went to Paris and took more classes at one of the oldest colleges in Europe. As his baseball career continued, so did his other interests away from baseball. He got traded to other teams, but he would always keep up his studies. He got into one of the best law schools in the country to become a lawyer. He skipped spring training that year so he could finish up with his classes.

Moe was a professional shortstop. But just two weeks into that season, his team (the Chicago White Sox) lost all three catchers to injury. Moe hadn't played catcher since he was just a kid out in the street but volunteered anyway. In his first game at his new position, they beat the Yankees. Babe Ruth was on that team and didn't get a single hit with Moe calling the pitches. He was now a catcher and wouldn't play another game in his career at any other position.

The next several years of his career were balanced between being a professional baseball player and being a Wall Street lawyer. He was injured a lot and didn't play much so he bounced around from team to team. He took advantage of an opportunity to go to Japan and help coach baseball teams there. This wasn't too long before World War II. The US wasn't on great terms with Japan. Moe quickly learned Japanese. And all on his own, he skipped a game claiming to be sick and went on his own sneaky mission.

In Tokyo, he went to a hospital pretending to be there to visit the US ambassador's daughter who had just had a baby. He got up to her floor, casually threw away the flowers he brought, and kept going up. He snuck up to the bell tower on the roof of the seven-floor hospital and pulled a camera out of the kimono he was wearing. He took pictures of military buildings and anything he thought might be useful to the United States.

Moe had found his true calling and it wasn't beating the Yankees and Babe Ruth although that had been fun. Soon after his time in Japan, he retired from baseball and got a job with the government organization that would eventually be known as the CIA or Central Intelligence Agency.

He went to "spy school" training and his final assignment was to sneak into a big army factory with lots of armed guards and steal some top-secret information. He did it. The former catcher was now officially an American spy.

World War II was now in full swing and Moe was sent to Europe with a gun, some money, and lots of black suits and ties (the uniform of a top-secret spy in those days). His job was to find out how close Germany was to building the Atomic bomb. He was to follow the top physicist in the world, the German scientist, Werner Heisenberg. He made friends with people in Switzerland who knew Heisenberg. Moe was invited by them to a lecture that Heisenberg was giving at a Swiss college. He was ordered to shoot to kill the famous scientist if he learned that the Germans were close to developing the Atomic bomb.

This was the top-secret spy job that Moe had been born for. He went to the college disguised as a student. He had two main things for this mission... his gun, and a poison pill that he would use to kill himself if captured by German soldiers. There were definitely Nazi soldiers there keeping Heisenberg under observation. But Moe didn't hear anything that night that was worth killing Heisenberg over. It sounded more to Moe as though the scientist didn't like the Nazis. But he would have to make sure. He got invited to a dinner that Heisenburg was going to where he found out that not only were the Germans not close to developing the bomb, but that they were losing the war. This was extremely useful information for the Allied forces in the war.

Moe was nominated for a top award for his work, the Medal of Freedom. But he declined it. Nobody knows why. He was very secretive. Years later, during the Cold War with Russia, he was sent to find out how close they were to developing Atomic bomb technology. He would sneak through checkpoints and really enjoyed being out in the field as a spy. But he didn't like having a boss or having to do things a certain way. His career as a spy wouldn't last much longer because of this. He was still a national hero for his work during World War II.

He would later die in a hospital when he was 70. He asked a nurse, "How are the Mets doing today?" and died before she could say anything. He never lost his love for baseball. And for me, Moe Berg is definitely one of the most interesting people to ever play the game.

Did the Lakers Really Draft a Cartoon Dog?

The NBA draft used to be really crazy and funny. The draft is where the teams in the league pick the best new players who are leaving college and starting their professional basketball careers. And in the 1970s and 1980s, teams used to make some especially weird picks.

Back then, there were as many as ten rounds of the NBA draft. There weren't enough good players to use all of those picks. The league would eventually reduce the picks that teams got in the draft. Today, there are only two rounds and 60 players selected. With a whopping ten rounds of draft picks, teams would run out of players that they actually wanted so they started having some fun with it.

In 1983, the Philadelphia 76ers drafted a 56-year-old pharmacist with the last pick in the draft. Apparently, he played cards with the owner of the team and they were friends. In 1984, the Chicago Bulls drafted Michael Jordan with their first-round pick. He would turn out to be the best player in league history. But with one of their final picks, they also drafted the Olympic track star, Carl Lewis, just for fun. Not only did Carl not play basketball in college, but he didn't even play in high school. So he wasn't too interested in going to the NBA. But that would seem like a pretty normal pick compared to some others I'm about to tell you about.

In 1974, the Atlanta Hawks picked a one-day-old baby with their 10th-round pick. Hmmm. The baby was pretty short and it definitely couldn't dribble a basketball. It couldn't even hold up its head! The wife of the Hawks executive who was picking all the new players had just had a child the day before the draft. The executive was Pat Williams. Pat eventually had 18 kids but only drafted the one to an NBA team. That kid never played in the NBA. Three years later, Pat's wife had another baby on draft day. But Pat had already drafted one baby and decided that was enough.

In 1977, it got even weirder. That was the draft that one of the league's most well-known franchises, the Boston Celtics, drafted their water boy with their final pick. Not to be outdone by their cross-country rival, the Los Angeles Lakers had two late picks. One, they actually used on a wooden chair. I'm not sure how that would have worked during a game. It might have been a little embarrassing to be pulled out of the game and replaced by a chair. They also tried to draft Scooby-Doo. Scooby was the cartoon dog hero who solved mysteries with his friends on television. I don't know if he was a very good basketball player. But Scooby was the first and last cartoon to be drafted by an NBA team.

A Historic Moon Shot

This was a moment like no other in all of human history. This had NEVER been done before. Millions of people were watching him. But he was so far away. There was a lot riding on this. He could really embarrass himself here if this didn't go well. He breathed deeply and settled in.

The year was 1974. And there was Alan Shepard, with a club in his hand getting ready to hit a golf ball. But he wasn't on a golf course or even the earth! He was on the moon. This would actually be the first time (and the only time) that any sport was ever played off of planet Earth.

Sixteen years earlier, Alan had been a Navy airplane pilot and was among the seven pilots that were chosen to be the very first astronauts by NASA. His invitation to try out for the assignment was actually misplaced and he didn't get an offer at first. But it all got worked out and he was accepted into the first group.

It was Alan who was chosen to be the first American into space. This was obviously a huge deal. Millions of people watched it on television. It's funny though, he wasn't even able to see the stars because of where the windows were placed. And he didn't get to float around in the spacecraft because he was strapped in really tight. But he was just the second person to ever fly in space (by a couple of weeks) and the first American.

That was in 1961. More flights went to space but Alan had already had his turn so he worked as support on the ground. Two years later, he would get another chance to fly into space. But one morning he woke up feeling sick and dizzy. He was crushed to find out that he had something called Mèniére's disease. This meant that fluid had built up in his inner ear which caused vertigo or dizziness. His career as an astronaut was over.

What good is a grounded astronaut? Plenty as it turns out. Alan became Chief of NASA's Astronaut Office which put him in charge of new astronaut training and gave him a role in space mission planning. Six years passed and he was able to undergo a surgery that fixed his ear. He was back to being flight-ready. His next assignment would be Apollo 13. You may have seen the Tom Hanks movie about it. The spaceship was damaged and they had to make a dramatic emergency flight back to Earth. Alan had actually been replaced on that flight and made commander of Apollo 14 so he wasn't on that dangerous Apollo 13 mission.

Finally, in 1971, Alan, who was the oldest astronaut there was at 47 years old, got his chance to get back into space. He got the idea to hit a golf ball up there and had to really work to convince his bosses that it was a good idea. But he was a persuasive guy. He also had to do a lot to prepare. It wouldn't be so easy swinging a golf club in a heavy, stiff astronaut suit. He needed practice and he needed to do it in secret so that his stunt would be a big surprise for the country.

He would put on his 200-pound spacesuit at a local golf course in Houston, Texas, and practice hitting balls out of the sand trap which would be similar to the surface of the moon. Because of how those spacesuits were made, he could only use one hand to swing the club. This would make it a difficult shot. And regular golf in shorts and a t-shirt is plenty difficult already! He would need a special club that would collapse into a smaller size so that it wouldn't take up too much room in the spacecraft. The golf pro at his practice course made one for him. It worked like a tent pole. Alan could fold it up and then unfold it and snap it together all into one piece. The club face was a 6 iron. Alan and his two crewmates spent 33 hours on the moon which was a new record. When they were ready to go, there was one final thing to do.

This would be the first full-color video transmission from space. Previous live television shots such as the very first landing on the moon were all in black and white. Alan told everyone back home watching what he was about to do. He lined up, and whiff! He hit only sand. He swung again...same result. This was tough. His crewmates were giving him some lighthearted teasing for doing so poorly. On this third try, he made contact with the ball but hit it off the end of the club face, shanking it into a nearby crater. It wasn't the shot Alan was hoping for.

Fortunately, he had taken more than one ball! Alan took one more swing. And it was glorious. He smacked the ball full-on and it flew up and stayed up for about half a minute before it floated down. Alan gleefully said, "Miles and miles and miles." But it actually only went about 200 feet, which was probably an extra 190 feet than it would have gone on earth being hit by a one-armed swing out of the sand. It didn't really matter how far it went. Everyone loved it. It became a huge news story and brought a lot of attention to NASA. It was a win for everyone. And the two balls he hit? They're still up there. Every now and then NASA will get a view of them from a passing satellite. And with those two golf shots, Alan Shepard left his mark on sports history.

Are These Late Game Heroics the Greatest in History?

It was senior night. There were 900 people in the stands. The auditorium at Greece Athena High School was jam-packed. Coach Jim Johnson had enjoyed a lot of success as a high school basketball coach in Greece, New York, just outside of Rochester. But his team, the Trojans, had never won a division title. Tonight was the big night. If the team won this game, they would for the first time...be division champions.

The crowd was electric. But they weren't just excited for the chance to celebrate their first division championship. Many were waving cut-out heads of their favorite player that they hoped to see that night. Only he really wasn't a player at all. But tonight he might finally get his chance.

His name was Jason McElwain, or J-Mac. He had never taken a shot for his team. He had never even gotten in a game. That's not because the coach was mean, J-Mac was the team manager. Every year he tried out for the team. And every year he was named manager instead of player. But he loved being the team's manager.

J-Mac was different. He had autism which meant it was impressive that he could even shoot a basketball at all. Autism is a disability that is caused by differences

in a person's brain. Jason was diagnosed with a severe case when he was little. Doctors don't know what causes autism but it makes it hard for people who have it to live a "normal" life. They can have trouble interacting socially and communicating. Jason's mom cried and cried when she got the diagnosis. But she was determined to give Jason the best life she could.

As a boy, he discovered basketball and became obsessed with it. He would shoot all day long in the summer. But he didn't make the junior high basketball team when he tried out. His mom called the school and begged them to let Jason be on the team. They did the next best thing. They let him be the team manager.

J-Mac worked really hard to support the team. He dressed up and wore a tie to every game. He loved the team and being a part of it, even if he couldn't play. That never stopped him from practicing. He would take 500 shots each and every day! He would tell his coach to give him a chance one day. So he worked to make sure he would be ready when that chance came. He loved basketball with all his heart.

At senior night in 2006, J-Mac had worked really hard for his team all these years and was finally in the 12th grade. The reason that so many of his fellow students had cut out pictures of J-Mac's face was that word had leaked out that tonight might be his big chance. Coach Johnson was going to try to get him into the game.

The coach was really nervous about this. He loved J-Mac and didn't know how he might react to the pressure of actually being out on the court. And it was such an important game for the team. He might not have the chance to let him play. However, the team was determined for J-Mac to have his chance. They all loved him too. They knew that for J-Mac to get on the court, the championship would have to be already decided. They needed to have a really big lead. They were playing the Spencerport Ranger Bears. But they had to do this for J-Mac.

The team fought as hard as they ever had. And they did it! They built up a big lead for their friend. With just over 4 minutes left in the game, coach Johnson looked over at J-Mac and told him to check in. When he got up and headed over to the scorer's table, the crowd went wild. This was it! They had no idea what was about to happen.

The kids at Greece Athena High School were special. They were so supportive of their classmate even though he was different. They were there to see his dream of playing for his high school come true. They got to witness so much more. Coach Johnson was thinking, "Please can we just get him a basket." J-Mac's teammates got him the ball. He shot. It was an airball that missed. He got another chance...and missed. It wasn't the best start, but he was playing.

Then...it happened. On his third try from the 3-point range, he buried it. The crowd went insane. This was J-Mac's big moment! People were crying. Everyone was so happy for him. But that's not where this story ends. He kept shooting, and he didn't miss another shot he took that night. He would put up 5 more 3-pointers. As each one swished through the basket, his teammates and the crowd went crazier and crazier. Nobody could quite believe what they were seeing. All of this in only 4 minutes of playing time!

Finally, the last seconds were ticking off the clock. As they did, J-Mac had the chance to put up one last shot. He was on fire. He had just scored 20 points in 4 minutes. As his shot went in and the final seconds ticked off the clock, he was swarmed. It was hard to watch it and not cry. I think it must be one of the happiest moments in sports of all time. Watching a kid who had worked so hard all his life and was so different from other kids, achieve something so incredible.

After that night, J-Mac and coach Johnson were on every big talk show in the country. The President flew in to meet them. It won ESPN's award for best sports moment of the year, beating Kobe Bryant's unbelievable 81-point night in the NBA. That's how special this was. It wasn't just a moment for that high school. It gave hope to autistic kids, their families, and anyone with a disability all over the world. It inspired EVERYONE. Jim Johnson hired J-Mac as a coach after he graduated and he's still on the sidelines of every Greece Athena High School basketball game. J-Mac's magical night lives on as one of the most epic moments to ever happen in sports.

A "Circus Puppet's" Revenge

Chess is one of the world's oldest and most popular board games that takes an incredible amount of skill and strategy to play well. Chess is considered a sport by the International Olympic Committee although it has not yet been played in the Olympics. The fun thing about chess is that sometimes girls compete against boys and young people compete against older people, sometimes with surprising results.

Like many things, chess was once and still is in some respects, dominated by men. It shouldn't be surprising that men used to think that women weren't as good as men at lots of different things. In chess, this was because girls and women had never really gotten the chance to compete or get chess training.

This is the story of one of chess's all-time great grandmasters and his dramatic defeat to someone he called a "circus puppet". That's not a very nice thing to call someone, is it? I'm talking about Garry Kasparov, the Russian World Chess Champion. He felt that women had no place in chess tournaments and didn't care who might have a problem with his opinion about it.

I should start at the beginning. This is really a story about Judit Polgàr. She grew up in the country of Hungary with her two older sisters. Her father felt that children could be trained to be masters of anything no matter if they were a girl or a boy if you started early enough. We now know that to become great at something, you don't always have to start it as soon as you can walk. But Judit's mother and father wanted to see if they could raise chess champions. So they trained all three daughters at it starting very early.

And it worked! Both of Judit's two older sisters (Susan and Sophia) became incredible chess players. Susan was the oldest, at 7 years older than Judit, and became the very first female grandmaster in chess history. At 15, Susan was the highest-rated female chess player in the whole world. Sophia was no slouch either as she became an International Master herself. But Judit was even more phenomenal. When she was just 5 years old she beat a family friend without ever glancing at the board.

Judit started playing in tournaments right after that. When she was 7, she and her 9-year-old sister Sophia, each played a game of chess blindfolded against two top chess masters. Both girls won! They kept playing. And they kept winning. They began traveling the world and people started to take notice of these little Hungarian girls who were somehow beating 50-year-old chess masters.

They refused to play in women-only tournaments as their father felt it ridiculous to separate women from men. And he was right. But when it came to team tournaments such as the Chess Olympiad where the players would represent their countries as a team, they could only play against women. The coach of the

Russian women's team arrogantly said, "I believe that these girls are going to lose a good part of their quickly acquired image in the 28th Olympiad...Afterward, we are going to know if the Hungarian sisters are geniuses or just women!" That male coach found out that the two Hungarian sisters were indeed both women AND geniuses. The Hungarian team of course won and Judit won best individual player in the tournament. She was 12 years old. This wouldn't be the last time she would make someone eat their words for underestimating her.

She was now rated as one of the top 100 chess players in the world. Judit was just the second woman to ever be rated that high. The first was her sister, Susan. Judit was only 12 years old. And she was just getting warmed up.

Her reputation continued to grow. A British grandmaster who lost a game to her called her a "cute little auburn-haired monster who crushed you." She was becoming known for her "killer eyes." Even her future nemesis, Garry Kasparov, took note. He was, of course, dismissive and said, "She has fantastic chess talent, but she is, after all, a woman. It all comes down to the imperfections of the feminine psyche. No woman can sustain a prolonged battle." But he would eventually find out for himself just how good she was.

At 15, Judit became the youngest chess grandmaster in history (boy or girl). She was only getting better and better. When she was 17, she faced Kasparov in a match for the first time. It resulted in a controversy. Kasparov moved his knight with his 36th move. He took his hand off the piece and realized he had made a mistake. He quickly moved the knight to a different square. Once a chess player takes their hand off a piece, their turn is over. They can't decide to put it somewhere else. This was Judit's very first tournament of this level. She had finally made it to play against the best of the best. But Kasparov, even though he broke the rules, was allowed to do it. He claimed his hand never left the piece. The videotape proved that it had. Even when tournament officials saw the video, they didn't change the result of the game like they were supposed to. Kasparov had won.

Judit confronted him about it after the game. Kasparov remained arrogant and told a journalist at the tournament, "... she just publicly said I was cheating...I think a girl of her age should be taught some good manners before making such statements." He was definitely not a fan of playing against Judit. He had already called her nothing more than "a circus puppet" and said that female chess players should focus on having babies, not playing chess. So he probably felt pretty good about himself after that first match. They would actually play several more times.

At 23 years old, Judit played in an elite tournament in Spain that only included the world's best six players. Kasparov was usually ranked as the very best in the world. And Kasparov would win this tournament. But in his two games against Judit, they would tie. And it was in these games that Judit felt like she figured out how to beat him. They would play again a year later. And she would be ready.

Judit had played Kasparov a total of 12 times. He had won 9 and they had tied 3 times. This would be their 13th match. Kasparov's lucky number was 13. He was born on the 13th day of April. And his place in chess history was that of the 13th world champion. He was feeling pretty sure of himself. He was ranked as the top chess player in the world. He was number one. And the tournament had started poorly for Judit. She lost her first two matches. This probably added to Kasparov's confidence. So he started the game with a different defense than he usually played. This would be his downfall. His arrogance showed and it cost him.

After 46 moves by Judit, it was clear that she had him. Kasparov was losing and he didn't like it one bit. He knew it was over. It was Judit's turn. But without looking at her he reached out his hand in resignation. They barely touched in a quick and feeble handshake, and he abruptly left the table and quickly escaped down a hallway where photographers couldn't follow him. He never looked Judit in the eye. She had done it. She was 24. She was a woman. And she had just defeated the best player in the world.

You're Not Allowed to Tie!

Can you tie for an Olympic Medal? It actually happens sometimes. If two winning competitors get the exact same time in a race, they would both get the gold medal and no silver would be awarded. The 3rd place finisher would get a bronze. But that doesn't happen very often because finishing times are measured to the hundredth of a second. In races, this makes ties very rare. But they've happened in all kinds of events for both men and women. There have also been ties in events where you are judged by a panel such as diving and even boxing.

Ties at the Olympics started all the way back in 1896 in Athens, Greece. That year, there was a tie for silver in the high jump, a tie for bronze in the pole vault, a tie for bronze in the 100-meter footrace, and even a tie for bronze in fencing. Since then, there have been ties in all kinds of events both in the Summer and Winter Games. There have actually been 151 ties for Olympic medals since 1896. But the Olympic Committees haven't always known how to deal with ties. Sometimes the rules are not in place, making final decisions difficult.

In 1936, the Olympics were held in Berlin, Germany. Hitler was in charge of Germany during this time and was trying to use the Olympics to spread his agenda on racism. The entire world was a bit on edge as everyone navigated these troubled times.

Japan sent two pole vaulters to compete in the men's competition. They were really good. Their names were Shuhei Nishida and Sueo Oe and they were good friends.

There were five pole vaulters left in the competition as the height they needed to jump kept getting higher and higher. 25,000 people were watching the final jumpers from the stands as the day turned to night. Of the five remaining pole vaulters, an American was the first to not make the jump and fall out of the competition. Another American, Earle Meadows, then made the gold medal pole vault by getting over the bar at 14 feet. He was the only one to get that high, so he had clinched the gold. That left three pole vaulters for silver and bronze. Next up was another American who didn't make it over the bar. The two friends from Japan, Shuhei Nishida and Sueo Oe were guaranteed a medal! They had both already made it over the bar at that height.

Since they had each made it over the bar, they were technically tied for silver. The Olympic Committee said they would have to each make another pole vault to see which of them would win the silver and which would settle for bronze.

Here's where it gets interesting. They refused to jump! Out of respect for each other, the two friends wanted to share the silver. And one of the first Olympic ties was actually in pole vaulting as I told you at the beginning of this story. But their desire to tie was turned down. The two jumpers didn't care, they still refused to jump again. The Olympic Committee told the Japanese team to make the decision. Because Shuhei had made the jump of 13.94 feet on his first try with Sueo getting it on his 2nd attempt which was allowed, Shuhei was given silver and Sueo was given bronze. They both looked pretty annoyed with this as they stood on the awards podium, Shuhei in the 2nd place spot and Sueo in the 3rd place position.

When they got back home, they did something special. They had their medals cut in half and then rejoined as each medal being half silver and half bronze. Nobody had ever done this before and nobody has done it since. These were the only two medals like this in the history of the Olympics. The medals became known by a special name, "The Medals of Friendship".

The two men had vaulted over the same height. They knew that they had tied. They didn't need anyone else telling them who was better. They decided for themselves. And they chose selflessness, humility, and sportsmanship. Even during an Olympics that had hate and insecurity trying to overshadow everything, there were many examples of sportsmanship and kindness that shined through. That's one of the things that we all love about sports. They offer a platform for great acts of humanity.

Not Much Could Stop the St. Paul Thunderbolt

This is the story of something amazing that happened inside a boxing ring a few weeks before Christmas in 1923. It starts with a really unlucky young boxer, Billy Miske...also known as the St. Paul Thunderbolt.

Just five years earlier, Billy was 24 and a really promising young fighter. He got his nickname because he was from Saint Paul, Minnesota. Billy had only been fighting for five years in 1918 and had already beaten a lot of boxing's all-time greats and former champions. But he got some terrible news from the doctor. Billy had Bright's disease. This meant that his kidneys were slowly failing him and the doctor said he needed to retire from boxing. Retire? He was just 24 years old! But much worse than that was that doctor told Billy he only had five years left to live.

Today, those kinds of kidney problems are no longer a death sentence. But unfortunately for Billy Miske, there weren't many treatment options in the early 1900s. What the doctor didn't know was that Billy couldn't possibly retire. He was broke. He wasn't just broke, he owed $100,000, which is like being a million dollars in debt today. Poor Billy had a car distributorship company in St. Paul. And it was NOT working. It was losing lots of money.

So Billy decided that not only would he keep fighting, but that he would keep his disease a secret. He probably had to in order to keep his fighting career going. So this tough fighter suffered in silence and kept fighting the very best of the best...with two bad kidneys. Your kidneys are two organs just below your rib cage. You have a left kidney and a right kidney. Boxers take lots of punches to the stomach and ribs. A boxer's kidneys take a lot of abuse. The fact that Billy kept fighting while having this disease makes him one of the toughest fighters of all time. But the story of his toughness is just getting started.

He would go on to step into the boxing ring 30 times after he was told that he should retire. He fought the famous Jack Dempsey for the heavyweight title in 1920. Dempsey was the best fighter in the world at that time. Billy had fought him to a draw two years earlier and then lost to him six months later. This would be his 3rd match with the great fighter and a championship was on the line. Dempsey punched Billy so hard in the chest that a big purple welt appeared right over his heart for everyone to see. Billy was knocked down by the punch and got up just in time to avoid a knockout. Dempsey was scared that he had killed Billy and didn't want to keep going but this was the St. Paul Thunderbolt! Billy kept fighting. He was relentless. But with a punch to the jaw, Dempsey knocked him out. It was the only time that Billy was knocked out in his entire career.

Three years passed with lots of fights for Billy. But now he really was dying. He looked awful and some days couldn't get out of bed. He had lost a lot of his old muscle and hadn't fought in almost a year. But Christmas was coming and he didn't have any money to buy his three children any gifts. He had paid back every penny of the $100,000 that he owed and had nothing left for his family. He needed one more fight. Billy knew his life was almost over. It was terribly unfair because he wasn't even 30 years old yet. But all Billy thought about was his kids. He wanted his last Christmas with them to be a good one. He asked his manager for a fight.

Jack Reddy had worked with Billy for years. He wasn't about to subject Billy to the humiliation of a boxing match when he couldn't even walk. And the fight might kill him! But Billy was persuasive and said he'd rather die in the ring than wait for death in his own bed. Jack caved in. But he didn't do Billy any favors with his matchup. He scheduled a fight with the feared Bill Brennan. Bill was a tough-as-nails brawler who had gone toe to toe with Jack Dempsey as well. It wasn't much of a step down from fighting Jack Dempsey himself. Fighting Bill Brennan in his condition seemed to be as much of a death sentence as Bright's disease.

Jack told Billy that he would have to get in shape and train for the fight. But Billy had no chance of doing any training. He barely left his bed leading up to his final fight. He didn't train at all. He couldn't.

It seemed unlikely he would even be able to make the trip to Omaha, Nebraska for the fight.

But somehow he did make the trip. And he walked into the ring for the first time in almost a year with no training time at all. Brennan was in shape. And he hit hard. The first round came and went. Billy was making it! He made it through the second round, and then the third. Finally, in the fourth round, Brennan hits the mat and didn't get up. Incredibly, it's a fourth-round miracle knockout for the St. Paul Thunderbolt! The date is November 7th, 1923. He had earned $2,400. And when his three children ran down the stairs that Christmas to see what Santa had brought them, there were presents everywhere. He even bought them a baby grand piano! They laughed and played all day. It was the best Christmas they had ever had.

That very next day, however, Billy called his manager Jack again. This time it wasn't to ask for another fight. Jack heard Billy say, "Come and get me, Jack. I'm dying." Jack got him to the hospital as quickly as he could. But there was nothing for the doctors to do. On New Year's day, less than two months after his last fight, Billy Miske was dead. This is an amazing story because of the toughness and determination that Billy showed even after he knew he was dying. His love for his family was enough to keep the talented boxer going until his body could go no further. This is the legacy of the St. Paul Thunderbolt, one of the toughest boxers to ever live.

The Secret Identity of a
Mysterious Golfer

This story happened in Hollywood, California in the 1930s. It's hard to believe that it's real. It seems much more like one of the movies that they make there. This is the story of the best golfer that nobody has ever heard of. Once upon a time in Hollywood...

Hollywood is where all the celebrities live, both today and back in the 1930s. And in the 1930s...many of them played golf. So if you were good at golf and involved in that scene in Hollywood, you would get to know a lot of famous people. That's what one golfer, John Montague, did. He became the club champion at Lakeside Golf Course and had the best golf score ever made on the course at the time. This meant that anybody who played there got to know him.

John was a man who enjoyed attention. And he got plenty of it. He was that good of a golfer. It was said that he had the longest drives anybody had ever seen. Back in those days, the clubs that golfers used were not nearly as fancy as the ones golfers use today. John's were made out of wood so it was much harder to hit a golf ball very far. Somehow he was able to. He was known all along the California coast as one of the best golfers alive. He was big and round, but short, with a New York accent. He was a "life of the party" kind of guy, always pulling pranks and making jokes. He became very well-liked because he was so funny.

He played a lot of golf with one of the most famous singers in the world at the time, Bing Crosby. Bing said that John was so good that he once knocked a bird off a telephone line...on purpose! Once, after Bing had lost one of his many games against John, he was complaining about it as he often did. John said they would play one more hole, giving Bing another chance to win. But...John would not play with his golf clubs. Instead, he would use a rake, a shovel, and a baseball bat. The hole was long at 366 yards. Bing got his ball with a chance to get it in the hole in just 3 shots but he missed the putt giving him a score of 4. John hit the golf ball out of the air with his bat and got it nearly all the way up to the hole, landing in a sand trap. He hit it out of the sand with the shovel onto the putting green. He was still 30 feet away from the hole though. He laid down on his stomach and used the handle of the rake like a pool cue and tapped the ball. It rolled into the hole for a score of 3. With antics like these, John's reputation really spread.

He had become very well known, but he never played professional tournaments. After playing with him, many professionals even considered John to be the best golfer in the world. Why wouldn't he compete for money? He always claimed that he played golf for "other reasons." Oh, and here's another thing. He never allowed his picture to be taken. Hmmm...most people can't wait to have their pictures taken with celebrities. But not John. If someone did happen to take his picture? He would make them destroy the film and give them $100 not to tell anyone about it. He also refused to talk to reporters. So what was going on here? That's what lots of people wanted to know.

One day, John was talked into playing with a sports writer who had secretly hired a photographer. He had the photographer hide in the bushes and sneak some photos. John found the photographer after the round and destroyed the film. But the photographer knew that might happen and had already replaced it with some blank film. The writer and the photographer sent the photos to *TIME* magazine. Uh oh.

Time was on magazine shelves all over the country. When a certain police detective in New York saw the photos, he thought he might have finally found the man he had been searching for all these years. Are you ready for this? It turns out that the reason that John Montague never played in professional tournaments was that John Montague...didn't exist! There was no such person. So who was this guy?

Are you ready for this? He was a fugitive, living with a fake name, on the run from the police! The New York police detective called the police in Los Angeles and they arrested John. It was then that John admitted to everything. The reason he had been so secretive was that his real name was LaVerne Moore. He was wanted for armed robbery back in New York.

This story quickly became a sensation. When he arrived at the train station in California for the three-day journey to New York, there were 100 people there clapping and cheering for him. His fame was just getting started. Reporters flocked to the trial to learn the story.

Seven years earlier, a restaurant was robbed by four masked men with guns. There was a car chase and two of the robbers crashed. Another car was pulled over with two men inside. They were smooth talkers and convinced the police that they weren't the robbers! A couple of days later, police figured out who they needed to arrest for the robbery. But by that point, LaVerne Moore had vanished!

The jury at the trial found LaVerne (John) not guilty! The judge was very disappointed because it was pretty clear that he was the 4th thief. But LaVerne was now a free man. He moved back to Hollywood and legally changed his name to John Montague. Now he was REALLY famous. Everyone wanted to meet him. His first public golf outing after the trial was with Babe Ruth, the famous baseball player. The crowds were so large that they quit playing at the 9th hole.

The interesting thing is that now that John Montague didn't have to hide anymore, his golf game completely fell apart. He tried to start a professional career but always struggled. He had become too famous. He had become too out of shape and overweight. The guy who was once the best golfer anyone had ever seen, fell apart when he no longer had to hide who he really was. But he had sure given everyone quite the show and a truly spectacular story.

Athletes Can Dance!

Could you imagine taking your favorite sports star to prom? How about a father-daughter dance? It's easy to forget that the athletes we cheer for (or against) on game day, lead lives of their own away from the sports they play. And so many athletes volunteer their time and money to support people who need it. One fun way that they do this sometimes, is by surprising people at a school dance.

Shaun White the famous snowboarder, showed up at a high school prom in Pennsylvania to surprise a young fan with his whole band and danced the night away with everyone. Dwayne Wade, the NBA all-star, Ronda Rousey, the UFC champion fighter, and JuJu Smith-Schuster, the Steelers wide receiver have all delighted and amazed lucky fans by going to school proms and giving them those special magical experiences. Don Jones took a girl with Down's syndrome to her high school prom when he played safety for the San Francisco 49ers. And I have to mention NFL receiver, Steve Smith, who was an autistic prom queen's date. That's a really sweet story as well. There are so many amazing and kind-hearted athletes.

There's one story that is especially moving. In March of 2021, 11-year-old Audrey Soape tragically lost her father. Just a few weeks later, her grandfather died. It was an awful and devastating year for her

family. Audrey's father had always taken her to the father-daughter dance at their church. This year, not only would he not be able to go, but even Audrey's grandfather wouldn't be there to fill in. So Audrey's mom took a long shot. The family was originally from Minnesota and were big Vikings fans. Their favorite player was Anthony Harris, who played free safety for the Vikings. Even after he became a Philadelphia Eagle, the family still rooted for him despite the family moving to Texas (this was Dallas Cowboy's country which is a bitter rival of the Eagles).

The family had even reached out from time to time on social media and the gracious star had always responded. Audrey's mom, Holly, knew that this was different. It was a lot to ask someone to fly across the country for this sort of thing. She said later, "I knew it was far-fetched and I didn't know what I was expecting, but I figured at least I would try." Anthony's team, the Eagles, were doing all they could to make the playoffs that year and he wasn't sure he could make it if they did. But he quickly responded to Holly and told her that he would do his best.

Anthony himself had been raised by a single mother. His heart was broken for his young fan. When it became clear that the Eagles would not make the playoffs, he reached out to the grieving wife and mother and told her that he would be honored to take young Audrey to the dance. Audrey's mom said that when Anthony told her he would come, "I was really blown away, it was just disbelief." Anthony didn't just come to the dance. He paid for Audrey to be able to get a new dress, and new shoes, and to go out and have her makeup and hair done for the big day. It was important to this NFL player that this girl he had never met, was made to feel special during the most difficult year of her young life.

On the day of the dance, Audrey was understandably really nervous! Anthony later laughed and said, "I think I might have been a little more nervous than she was." What helped immensely was that not only is Anthony one of the most kind-hearted people you could ever hope to meet, but he is also incredibly nice and charming. He immediately made the entire family feel comfortable and worked really hard to make Audrey feel special. Audrey said that "it didn't feel like I was with someone that was in the NFL, it felt like I was with a normal person that was my friend."

That night they danced. They laughed. It was a really special evening for everyone there when it could have been really painful. Anthony showed Audrey that even though she had suffered, she was supported. She would be okay. She would make it. When you lose someone you love, it's easy to feel alone. It's easy to feel abandoned. Anthony said "I just wanted to try to help her cope through that experience without her father being there...I had people in my life, sometimes complete strangers, that were very supportive of me, so I wanted to do that for her." Audrey's mom said, "When you see someone show up for your kid to make them feel special, to make them feel unique, it was just so unbelievably touching for me."

Professional athletes are often under a lot of pressure. They have to train and work really hard to be so good at what they do. Many of them somehow also make the time to support the fans and communities that support them. It's incredibly touching when they do. I don't know about you, but I think I have a new favorite NFL player. As people on this planet, we really are all in this together. Thank you Anthony Harris, for reminding us.

The All-Star Arrested for Cruelty to Animals During a Game

It was the 11th inning with two outs. There were base runners on first and 2nd base. This was game 6 of the World Series. If they could somehow win this game, they would be champions. As he walked to the plate he had to put out of his mind his past World Series performance. This was "Mr. Jay", the Blue Jays veteran superstar and future hall of famer, Dave Winfield. Eleven years earlier was the only other time he had played in a World Series and it was a disaster. He was playing for the New York Yankees then. That's some serious pressure. Despite being one of the Yankees' best players during the regular season, he only had one hit in the entire World Series. That was out of 22 at bats! It was dreadful. And then he committed a costly error in game 6 that helped them lose the series. The Yankees owner insultingly started calling him "Mr. May" which meant he was good when it didn't matter early in the season, and terrible in October when it was crunch time in the playoffs. The Yankees also had Reggie Jackson on that team and his nickname was Mr. October thanks to his heroic playoff and World Series performances.

But eventually "Mr. May" became "Mr. Jay" and would finally have the chance to put all of that behind him. But playing so terribly in the 1981 World Series for the Yankees wasn't the weirdest thing to happen to Dave Winfield while he played in New York. Two years later, is when *IT* happened...probably the strangest thing to ever happen to Dave Winfield in his life. The Yankees were playing in Toronto, Canada against the same Blue Jays that Dave would eventually play for. It was the bottom of the 5th inning and before play started the guys were warming up by tossing a ball around. It was now time for play to start, so Dave threw the ball back to the dugout. Toronto is a coastal city on Lake Ontario and at the time, Exhibition Stadium was right by the water. This meant that seagulls were always a common sight around the stadium, especially on game day. Fans watching the game meant peanuts, popcorn, and all kinds of tasty treats for the birds.

When Dave tossed the ball to the dugout, it hit a seagull and killed it. He was 80 feet away from it! This was a fluke accident. But Blue Jays fans were outraged. They thought that he had hit the bird on purpose. The Blue Jays hated the Yankees, which may have had a hand in what happened after the game. When Dave went to the locker room, the police were there and they arrested him for cruelty to animals. I'm 100% all in support of protecting animals from mean people, but this? Ridiculous! Dave's coach and team manager, Billy Martin, joked, "That's the first time Winfield's hit the cutoff man all year." But Billy was really angry that his player was actually arrested and said, "I'll tell you one thing. When Toronto comes down to New

York next week, we're going to get their four starting pitchers arrested."

What a mess! The Blue Jays general manager was embarrassed and paid Dave's fine of $500 at the police station himself. He also drove Dave to meet back up with his team since the arrest caused him to miss the team bus. The Blue Jays President would later drive to New York to give Dave an apology in person. Blue Jays fans may have thought it was funny but most people in Toronto thought it was quite silly. The police actually had an autopsy performed on the seagull to determine the cause of its death! It seemed pretty clear that it was the ball that had done it, but the autopsy found that the bird was sick and would have died soon anyway, which further validated how silly this arrest was. One TV anchor in Toronto said that Dave had three hits in the game, "Two baseballs and a seagull."

For years after this incident, anytime Dave had to play in Toronto (which was a lot because they were in the same division with the Yankees) they would always make seagull noises and flap their arms like wings when it was his turn to bat. Dave was a pretty good sport about the whole thing and the charges were dropped the next day. After the season, Dave actually went back to Toronto for a fundraiser to help the disabled. What did he bring for the auction? A painting of seagulls, of course! It raised $32,000 for the good cause.

So all of this made it especially interesting when Dave ended up signing a contract to play for the Blue Jays. It had been 8 years since that fateful day with the seagull. Dave was 40 years old now which is pretty old for a baseball player. But he was still playing great and won everyone over in Toronto. He became a fan favorite and when he stepped up to the plate in game 6 of the 1992 World Series, he probably wasn't thinking at all about that seagull. He had turned 41 by this time. Dave was 0 for 4 in this game. He hadn't gotten a hit. On the 6th pitch of the at bat with two runners on in the 11th inning with all the pressure on him, Dave delivered a smash down the left field line that would score both runners. He had won the game! He had won the World Series! And he had become the 3rd oldest player in baseball history to hit an extra-base hit in the World Series. But Dave's was special. It was the series winner.

The incident with the seagull was now completely forgotten. So were his World Series struggles from 1981 with the Yankees. Dave was Toronto's hero. He had delivered the city and the franchise their first-ever World Series championship. Even the seagulls were happy.

When Muhammad Ali Stopped a Guy From Jumping Off a Building

At one time, Muhammad Ali was the most famous person in the world. Nobody else was even close. Throughout his life, he was one of the most charismatic, larger-than-life characters that anyone could ever hope to meet. There had never been anyone like him and there hasn't been anyone like him since he lived. As a boxer, he won three championships on *three different* continents! Both his career and his personal life are the stuff of legend. But this is the story of the day that he got a strange phone call.

First, let's dive into the kind of person he was. When Muhammad was rich and famous, he once had $5,000 in his pockets and someone pickpocketed him and stole it. That's a lot of money to carry around! His manager couldn't believe it and was getting on to him about how he shouldn't do that and how irresponsible it was to carry that much money in his pockets. Muhammad said that he just helped someone who really needed it and that $5,000 probably went to pay someone's rent for a year. Someone was better off. He had a generous heart. As the most famous person in the world, there were lots of demands on his time and he was constantly getting asked for autographs and to take pictures with people. Once, he was late for a plane and was running through an airport to catch it so it didn't take off without him. But a woman yelled his name. His manager couldn't believe it. Muhammad was stopping to talk! Muhammad would later explain that it was that woman's only chance she would ever have to meet him. And to him, it was only a moment. But to her, it was important. And he would ALWAYS have the time to talk to anyone who wanted to talk or take a picture with him.

Later in his life when Parkinson's disease made it nearly impossible for Muhammad to sign his name for people quickly, he would sit at home and sign pictures. He would carry 1000s of those pictures with him in a bag so he wouldn't have to tell people that he couldn't give them an autograph. When Muhammad was a little boy, he waited all day to get a famous boxer's autograph. When he finally saw the boxer and ran up to him, the boxer said, "Get away from me, kid." Muhammad was devastated and carried that with him for the rest of his life. He was always determined that nobody would ever feel that way because of him. There are so many great examples of what a great humanitarian he was. But let's jump to a Monday in Los Angeles, California, on January 19, 1981.

A depressed and unhappy man stepped out onto the ledge of an office building. He wanted to jump from nine floors up and end his life. A crowd had gathered down below to see what would happen. The police had spent hours trying to talk him down. They had called in a priest, as well as a psychologist, but nothing was working. Muhammad's best friend, Howard Bingham, happened to walk up and saw what was happening. Howard knew that Muhammad would want to help so he called him. Fortunately, Muhammad was only four minutes away. Muhammad got there as fast as he could. He had to drive down a wrong-way street in his Rolls Royce with his hazard lights flashing. The Champ had arrived.

Here's the thing about Muhammad Ali. He was a great pitchman. He could whip up a crowd and knew just how to talk to reporters to get people interested in a fight. But one thing he didn't do was draw attention to the nice things he did for people. He did these things nearly every day. 1981 was the year that Muhammad would retire from boxing. He was dealing with the early stages of Parkinson's disease. He was having tremors and twitches on his face and hands. He was even starting to slur his words because the disease was making it harder to talk. So he wasn't spending as much time in public because of these symptoms. What happened on this fateful day was not a publicity stunt. It was simply Muhammad doing what he did every day...being a hero.

The police led him right up to the unhappy man. He was The Champ after all. This was Muhammad Ali! "Yes sir, I'll take you right there." Muhammad stuck his head out of a window so he could see the potential jumper, whose name was Joe. Muhammad yelled out to the man, "You're my brother! I love you, and I couldn't lie to you." Muhammad might have been the only man in the world that Joe would have let near him. Joe let him come to him through the fire escape to put an arm around him. Joe told Muhammad that he was a nobody and that everyone had always told him he was a nobody. He didn't feel important. But it was impossible for anyone to feel unimportant around Muhammad Ali. Muhammad made him feel special. And when they got off that 9-story ledge, the police started to chant, "USA! USA! USA!" Muhammad drove Joe to the police station in his Rolls Royce and checked in on him several times after that.

People who needed strength could always get it from Muhammad Ali, one of the greatest athletes to ever live. That's the power that our sports heroes have. Muhammad Ali always gave of himself every chance he had. Whether he was fighting in the ring or fighting for the powerless. He was known as "The People's Champion." He was not a perfect person (nobody is) but he always lived up to that nickname. And on that day in 1981, he was more than a sports hero. He was a real-life superhero saving the life of someone who really needed help.

This Texas Rancher Had the Greatest Season in NFL History

I'll bet you haven't even heard of the guy who DOMINATED the NFL and at one time was the best quarterback in the league as well as the best safety in the league, and also the best punter. Surely you'd know about an NFL player like that, right? This guy, in one magical season, led all of professional football in passing yards, punting yards, AND catching interceptions as a defensive back! He's the only person to ever do that and in today's game that record is basically impossible to ever beat.

But get this! In one game alone he threw for four touchdowns. So? Big deal. That happens all the time. But in that same game, he also intercepted four passes by the other quarterback and kicked an 81-yard punt. Sounds like a video game doesn't it? But this was real life. If you could mash up Tom Brady, with Ron Woodson, with Shane Lechler...you might have the legendary Slingin' Sammy Baugh.

So who in the world was this guy? He was in the very first class of players to be inducted into the Hall of Fame and one of only two who received 100% of the votes. It's easy to see why. It's been a little bit since he played. So I'll forgive you for not knowing who he is. Sam Baugh's heyday was back in the 1930s and 40s.

The games weren't even on television then. You might be thinking, yeah that's cool and all but wasn't the game a lot easier back then? You'd be wrong. Dead wrong. Sam was the first quarterback to play the position as it's played now, doing things like passing on first down. You might think, "Well no wonder he led the league in passing!" But here's an interesting tidbit. The footballs in Sam's day were much harder to throw because they were a different size. They were rounder and harder to get your hand around. It didn't fly as far through the air because of its shape and it was heavier. Also, defensive players could just tackle receivers to keep them from catching the ball. There was no such thing as pass interference. Yet, his numbers and stats were still crazy.

He STILL has the record for most seasons leading the NFL in passing. Nobody has done that for more than six seasons like Sam did, although Steve Young tied the record. Sam also still has the record for most seasons with the lowest interception percentage for quarterbacks. He did for five seasons despite throwing for the most yards. And Sam's average yards per punt in a single season of 51.4 yards is a record that no punter has beaten for over 80 years! But I think his craziest and most impressive record is leading the league in passing, punting, and catching interceptions in a single season. He never came out of games and was the best at anything he did.

Sam was obviously an incredible athlete. He and his 3 brothers grew up with a single mother deep in the heart of Texas. And what he really wanted was to become a professional baseball player. Baseball was much more popular than football then. He had a baseball scholarship to go play at Washington State but hurt his knee on a slide into 2nd base and lost the scholarship. He was allowed to play three sports (basketball, baseball, & football) while going to Texas Christian University and helped them win the Cotton Bowl and the Sugar Bowl. In 1936, Sam was 4th in the Heisman Trophy voting. He was a 1st round draft pick for the football team in Washington DC. At that time, they were called the Redskins. As a rookie, he was the team's highest-paid player with a contract for $8,000. That's a bit less than rookie quarterbacks make today, but a lot of money in 1937.

Even still, Sam wasn't sure he wanted to play football. He actually signed a contract with the St. Louis Cardinals first and gave that a try. It didn't work out so he thought he'd give that football thing another try and ended up smashing all of the NFL records and becoming the most dominant and popular player in the league. In one championship game, he threw for 335 yards which was a playoff record for *75 years* until Russell Wilson threw for 388 yards in a playoff game in 2012.

After retiring, Sam got into acting and played a Texas ranger lawman on TV. He was the original Chuck Norris. (If you don't know, Chuck Norris was the awesome action star with the hit TV show *Walker Texas Ranger*.) But mostly Sam worked on his own ranch. Today, his son operates the 20,000-acre Texas ranch. Amazingly, Sam said that if he could live life all over again, he never would have played football. He would have just ranched instead because he enjoyed that more than anything else he ever did. He was probably even better at ranching than he was at football, they just don't keep stats for ranching. But we can be certain that there has never been an NFL player quite like Slingin' Sammy Baugh.

LeBron, the Myth, the Man

LeBron James. He's currently one of the most iconic athletes on the planet. Some people love him, some people can't stand him. It was that way with Kobe Bryant and Michael Jordan, as well. Here are some interesting stories about him that you may not know. When LeBron was born, his Mom was only 16. So things were tough with such a young mom. She loved him very much, but his Dad wasn't around. That makes things really tough, too. They couldn't afford to buy the expensive basketball shoes. This is why it means a lot to LeBron when he gets shoes named after him by a big company like Nike. He always remembers what it was like to be too poor to have a nice pair. To get him out of the rougher parts of Akron, Ohio, his Mom let him stay with his basketball coach who was an important role model in his life. LeBron started playing basketball when he was in the 5th grade.

When LeBron played for his high school in 9th grade, his team was the only team in Ohio to go undefeated. When he was in 11th grade he was put on the cover of *Sports Illustrated* magazine! He also played wide receiver for his high school's football team. He was really good at that, too and lots of colleges wanted him to come play for them. The first time his high school basketball team played on national TV, everyone wanted to see LeBron. But he knew that was a great chance for his teammates to get some attention, too. So he worked really hard to pass the ball and help his teammates have a good game so that they would have a chance to play in college. LeBron could have made it all about him and scored 50 or 60 points if he had wanted to. But he was a teammate first and his friends loved him for it.

He always tried to be a good teammate. In the 8th grade, LeBron was playing in a tournament championship and his team was getting beat by around 20 points. Can you believe that? Basketball players often foul the best player...a lot. LeBron took a really hard foul and was on the ground for several minutes. His teammates knew they had to keep going even if LeBron couldn't play. They actually came back from being down 20 points and tied the game. It went into overtime. LeBron came back in the game and dominated overtime. His team won by 10 points with him scoring nearly all of them. He told his team on the way home, "I couldn't feel my arm or leg for a minute. But I knew I had to get back out there and help. I had to do something."

Another fun LeBron story is when he went to Nike headquarters and played a game of PIG. PIG is the same as HORSE, just shorter. If you make a shot and the person you're playing against misses, then they get a letter. And the first person to miss 3 shots that the other makes, loses. LeBron agreed to play someone from Nike in a game of PIG. The employees had their own PIG tournament to decide who would play the game against LeBron. Ros Gold-Onwude was an intern at Nike. But she was also a basketball player at Stanford which is one of the best women's college basketball programs in the country. Ros didn't even enter herself into the competition, a friend of hers did. On that day she wasn't wearing basketball clothes, she had gone to work in sandals and a yellow dress. She beat all the other Nike employees and would face LeBron. Everyone thought it was really fun that a girl in a dress was the best basketball player there. Ros actually got a lead on LeBron, too! After the game, LeBron signed a lot of basketballs and handed them out, and made sure to toss one to Ros. Some other guy jumped out of the crowd and grabbed it but LeBron made him give it to Ros.

Another time, LeBron was at a red carpet movie premiere. These are fancy events when a new movie comes out. LeBron walked right by Caron Butler and his daughter without saying anything. Caron played in the NBA for 14 years and had played against LeBron quite a bit. It was crowded and LeBron only realized after he had walked by that it was Caron. So he walked all the way back around the crowd to say hello to Caron and his family. Caron's daughter who was 7 years old, asked her dad, "Dad, you know LeBron James?" Caron really appreciated that from LeBron. He later said "I'll never forget that and my kids will never forget that...It was special. Man, I got points for that one. For people to go out of their way, I'm telling you about 85-90 percent of the guys who are superstars, or guys that are not even superstars, wouldn't think that's important. He's different. He really is. He's a different cat."

LeBron always works hard to make people feel special. That can be hard to do when you're one of the most famous people in the world. Everyone wants your attention. So it takes a special person to know that you should be nice to everyone and do all that you can for people. He's always doing that. Once, he met an interviewer at a hotel lobby and they accidentally found themselves at a wedding ceremony. LeBron and the interviewer spoke for almost an hour on a little balcony, but as guests started to arrive for the wedding they all started to notice that LeBron James was there. So of course, LeBron just walks out there and everyone raises their glasses to toast him. LeBron was in the playoffs at the time and said to the bride and groom so that everyone at the wedding could hear, "You're getting rings, I'm getting a ring." And then took pictures with the couple getting married. That's who LeBron is. He's also the guy who works really, really hard to be a champion and the best player in the NBA.

In the 2016 finals, his Cleveland Cavaliers were down 3 games to 1. That meant that if they lost one more game it was all over. They would have to win 3 straight games to be NBA champions. LeBron told them, "If you don't believe that we can win, don't get on the plane." To be able to win, you have to believe that you can do it. LeBron knew this. He helped his teammates understand that and they did come back to win the championship that year and most of them credit LeBron's talk as the reason they were able to turn the series around. LeBron had done that before. Before he had ever won a championship he played for the Miami Heat. They were down 2 games to 3 in the Eastern Conference Championship. Whoever won would go to the finals. At that time, everyone thought that LeBron couldn't play under the pressure of the big games. Nobody gave the Heat any chance at all. But young LeBron stopped everyone before they got on the plane for that next game. He told every player that "If you don't have 100 percent faith that we win this game, if you're not coming in here for a war, if there's nothing else on your mind don't come on this plane." Not only would the Heat win the next two games against the Celtics, but they would win their first championship that year. What LeBron said in both of those moments is how champions think. But it's how champions treat people every day that really shows you who they are. LeBron James isn't just an NBA champion. He's a champion human being. And that's why people love him.

The Endurance Athlete Who Inspired Homeless Kids to Dominate

Imagine yourself looking out at the waves of Redondo Beach in California as the sun begins to dip below the horizon. Night is coming quickly. Sunset is one of the prettiest times of day at the beach. But Jamshid Khajavi isn't here to relax. The 66-year-old Iranian-born man in his speedos walks out to the water and positions his goggles. His skin glistens with the greasy vaseline that he rubbed on to help keep him warm in the cold water. With the sun setting, he will begin the 21-mile swim through the shark-filled Pacific waters to Catalina Island. He'll swim all night and most of the next day. If he makes it, he'll have done it 5 times. The fact that it's been over 20 years since he last did it doesn't faze him one bit. And this might be one of the least crazy things that Jamshid has done in a while.

Jamshid isn't just a swimmer. He's an ultra-distance athlete. He's a runner, too. For the past 35 years, he has gone all over the world to run races that are 100 miles long. He swam the Straits of Gibraltar...twice! That's the stretch of the Mediterranean Sea that separates Africa from Europe. He's also swam around Manhattan Island in New York City a bunch of times. He's peddled a bicycle all the way across the country from California to New York, coast to coast. It took him 31 days. He has pulled a sled for 100 miles in temperatures below zero in the Alaskan ultra race, the Susitna 100. He didn't just do it once. He's done it *eighteen* times! He's run in 100-mile races through the world's hottest deserts and highest mountains.

Want to hear the REALLY crazy thing? These aren't even the coolest things that you're about to learn about Jamshid. The impact that he has had on others is much, much bigger than his endurance sports accomplishments. Jamshid is retired now and devotes all of his time to being in nature and his crazy feats of endurance. But for 39 years, he worked as a school counselor inspiring young kids. He's worked at schools in San Diego and Seattle. Jamshid was always drawn to schools in really poor areas with lots of problems. These kids needed him the most. But they weren't really sure about all the weird sports ideas that Mr. Jamshid had.

Mr. Jamshid had an idea. There was this prep school ultimate frisbee tournament. Prep schools are usually for kids in 6th grade through 12th grade. Some prep schools are really expensive! So you usually have to be from a wealthy family to attend a school like this. But this wasn't just any prep school frisbee tournament. This was Spring Reign, the biggest ultimate frisbee tournament...in the entire world. Ultimate frisbee is a team sport that is a mix of soccer and football but with a frisbee. You have two end zones and have to move the frisbee by throwing it to teammates. If it hits the ground the other team gets to grab it and move it up the field. When you catch it in the endzone, that's a score. You can't run with the frisbee, you have to catch, stop, and throw. It's really fun. Most schools don't have ultimate frisbee teams. But some wealthy prep schools do. You want to know who else has an ultimate frisbee team? Bailey Gatzert Elementary school, the school where Jamshid works.

This school and this team were not like the others at the Spring Reign tournament. Bailey Gatzert is in downtown Seattle. It's one of Seattle's poorest inner-city schools. And it's an elementary school, Kindergarten up to 5th grade. Spring Reign was a tournament for middle schools and high schools. And Gatzert's ultimate frisbee team? It was made up of kids from Seattle and some of the students are also refugees from Ethiopia or other African countries. Many of them were so poor that they didn't have homes to live in. But they had Jamshid Khajavi. Jamshid said that it was probably always around half of his team that were living in homeless shelters. He said, "When you're not sure where you're going to sleep at night, a Frisbee team can become a form of survival. The games have intense meaning to them."

Jamshid had students at Gatzert Elementary doing all kinds of sports like stair climbing, ping pong, and even yoga practice. The kids loved it. When Jamshid was there, his students would also compete in the Columbia Tower run. This was a race upstairs, 69 floors of them. Jamshid's teams won the elementary school division 15 years in a row. He would teach them and train them at recess and lunch every day. When he first got to the school Jamshid said that "...we couldn't play sports here at all because the kids were fighting so much." He wanted to find ways to teach them self control and confidence.

Back to the Spring Reign tournament. These homeless kids, these refugee kids from other parts of the world...dominated. One parent from another team said, "Our team was soundly thrashed by this completely unknown team, all of whose girls (wore) headscarves and long skirts. One of them was barefoot. Usually, the rich private teams like University Prep or north end schools are the strongest players at this event. There is something special going on here." She was right. Something special *was* going on. Jamshid's team won the tournament 4 out of 7 years against teams with players who were 2 or 3 years older than the Gatzert kids.

It doesn't matter where you come from or how much money your family has. Sports is the great equalizer. All that matters is how well you can play. Jamshid dedicated his life to helping kids who really needed help. The impact he was able to have may carry on forever through all the lives that he helped change. That night on Redondo Beach, he would swim for 10 hours but fail to make it across the channel because of unusually rough seas. But Jamshid never shies away from the possibility of failure. It once took him 30 hours to swim across the channel but because he landed on a jetty that was man-made, it didn't count for the record books. Still, he keeps going. Just as he did for all those kids that he helped over his 39-year career as an "active adventure counselor". He still hopes to be the oldest person to swim across if he can do it as a 70-year-old in 2023. I wouldn't bet against him. Jamshid says that his Iranian heritage gave him a special attitude that has always helped him. "In my culture, we have a different perspective on life and death. This is a short life, so we should do the best we can for each other and the environment and enjoy every minute." Well said, Jamshid. Well said.

The Only Dead Jockey to Ever Win a Horse Race

This story is as weird as it is sad. Perhaps because it happened 99 years ago, we can laugh about it just a little. All kinds of weird stuff happened in the world back in the 1920s. It was a very different time. But there certainly weren't zombie jockeys out racing horses. This is about when, at the prestigious Belmont Park racetrack in New York, one unlucky jockey won a steeplechase horse race while he was dead. What a show-off!

Belmont Park is found just east of New York City. It was opened in 1905 and ever since, has been one of the premier horse racetracks in the world. In June of 1923, Frank Hayes was getting ready for his big day. Frank was 22 years old and had never won a race in his life. But it's not because he was a bad jockey, he had only raced once before! Frank immigrated from Ireland to New York and worked in horse stables as a trainer, not a jockey. But the glory of actually winning on top of the horse you've trained looked like a lot of fun to Frank. So he gave it a try and his second race would be a big one. It would be at the famed Belmont Park.

Even in 1923, Belmont Park was a really big deal. The Wright brothers had flown there in their plane during a big show. And it had become the last race in the Triple Crown a few years earlier in 1919. The

Triple Crown is the set of 3 races that starts with the Kentucky Derby, includes the Preakness Stakes in Maryland, and finishes with the Belmont.

So there was young Frank getting ready for just his second race and it was at the famous Belmont. He must have been pretty nervous. To be a jockey you can't weigh very much. The less you weigh, the faster your horse can run. Frank didn't weigh much for a 22-year-old but lost even more weight now that he was a jockey. He had just gone from 142 pounds down to 130 pounds. Doing that quickly can be hard on your body, but he wanted to win.

Frank would be racing his own horse Sweet Kiss in the steeplechase. The steeplechase was (and still is) a kind of race where you have to jump over fences, bushes, and pits. It started in Ireland so Frank would have been very familiar with it. This steeplechase race at the Belmont was two miles long. Not only did your horse have to be fast, but it needed to be a good jumper as well. To be a good jumper, the horse needed to be brave. It had to jump those big bushes without knowing exactly what was on the other side. Lots of steeplechase riders fell off their horses going over these jumps.

Frank and Sweet Kiss were ready. They had a fantastic race. They stayed in the lead pack the whole way around the track. It was a close race with just a couple of jumps left. That was the point that Frank seemed to get really relaxed. He was riding with only one hand holding the reign and was slumped down in the saddle. Hmmm, that's weird. Must be a cocky kid. People thought that

Frank was showing off. He went over a couple of jumps riding that way. After they were done with the jumps, they came around the final turn for the sprint to the finish line. Frank and Sweet Kiss crossed the finish line in a close finish but they had won!

When officials walked over to congratulate the young man on his first win, Frank slid out of the saddle and landed in the dirt. He was dead. It was determined that he had a heart attack during the race. This could have been because of a couple of things. Losing all of that weight so quickly probably put extra strain on his heart. Maybe the excitement added to it. Maybe Frank didn't have the strongest heart to begin with and the race and the weight loss were just too much for it. The judges had no idea what to do. Do they award the race to a dead man? Or do they pronounce the 2nd place finisher the winner because that guy was at least still alive?

They decided to award Frank the win and not count it against him that he was dead when he crossed the finish line. It's really amazing that his body stayed on the horse, especially through a couple of jumps! The whole thing is quite bizarre. Frank Hayes is still the only person known to have won an official horse race while dead. Hopefully, that record doesn't ever get matched. It's a shame because Frank didn't deserve an ending like that, but it does add a fascinating element to sports and horse racing history. Nobody ever raced Sweet Kiss again because they thought the horse must be unlucky. The poor horse didn't do anything wrong but became known forever after as Sweet Kiss *of Death*.

Roller Derby Queen

If you were asked to pick the highest-paid female sports athlete in the 1960s what sport would you pick? Maybe a female tennis player or a softball team member? Wrong. The highest-paid female athlete in the United States in the 1960s was Joan Weston, also known as the Roller Derby Queen.

Roller Derby was born in the 1930s. It's competitive roller skating at its finest, featuring two teams of up to 15 players each. Each team puts 5 skaters on the track. One skater is the jammer and their job is to get around the other team's players to score points. The jammer wears a star on their helmet. The other four players are called the blockers. They try to prevent the other team's jammer from getting around them. The early days of this sport were highly theatrical and quickly gained loyal roller derby fans.

Joan Weston came along at just the right time and was just what the sport needed. At 5'10" with long blonde hair, this California girl was an incredible athlete. She played softball for her school and once scored 8 home runs in just one game! But mostly, Joan loved to roller skate. She said that skating along at 30 miles per hour gave her an incredible sense of freedom.

When she started roller derby, she had a bit of a learning curve to overcome. The roller derby crowd was known for being a bit rough around the edges.

Joan, who had attended private school and led a very sheltered life didn't know what to make of these people. She toughened up, but she kept her good girl image throughout her career.

At her first scrimmage, Joan had a bout of clumsiness, falling and knocking down 9 other skaters. That's not a great start! Luckily, she quickly got the hang of things and soon got offered to skate with the San Francisco Bay Bombers. She became known as the Blonde Bomber and the fans loved her.

She eventually became the captain of the Bombers. This is where she would meet her nemesis. Ann Calvello didn't like Joan and she didn't have any problem showing it. She would use any opportunity to provoke Joan's team, sometimes throwing illegal kicks and punches. Joan would fight back and the biggest rivalry in roller derby was formed. Fans loved it and would pack into the seats to see what drama would unfold next.

Once when Joan was arguing with a referee, two of her teeth flew out and over the ref's shoulder! Trips to the dentist for dentures and missing teeth were pretty common for a roller derby player back in those days.

At its peak, there were over 5 million roller derby fans. Even though it was not considered one of the major sports, Joan did very well and managed to be the highest-paid female athlete at the time. Even with her incredible popularity, she was still paid $20,000 less than the leading male roller derby player.

Joan skated as a professional for 19 seasons. It was a tough life, with plenty of miles traveling to different cities and lots of time away from home. But her love of roller skating and the sport of roller derby kept her going. When she retired, she helped to train young skaters and manage exhibition games. As one of the most incredible athletes of her time, Joan was a role model to other athletic girls and helped them find a sense of belonging.

The Tiny Med Student Who Saved Notre Dame's Championship Season

Reggie Ho is from Hawaii. His father was a doctor and he wanted to follow in his father's footsteps. He was a very smart kid. He also kicked field goals for his high school football team. He got accepted into the University of Notre Dame to study medicine. That's hard to do. You need to have really good grades. And once you're at college to become a doctor, you have to study. A LOT. It's really hard work. But Reggie wasn't afraid of hard work. This is yet another spectacular story of the unlikeliest of heroes.

Notre Dame is a long way from Hawaii. But it is known as a prestigious university with a really good pre-med program. When Reggie was a freshman, he got all A's. He was a determined student. But he spent all his time in the library studying. It occurred to him that college was his chance to learn all kinds of things and that it was important to be a well-rounded person. So what else could he do?

Most people would not have suggested football. Notre Dame had one of the best teams in the country full of the very best scholarship athletes around. And Reggie was small. Really small. He was only 5 feet and 5 inches tall and only weighed 135 pounds. Even kickers were usually much bigger than that. But that didn't bother Reggie. He decided that he would try out for the football team.

In 1986, Notre Dame had a brand new coach, Lou Holtz. Nobody knew it at the time, but Coach Holtz would become one of the best college football coaches in the history of the sport during his 10 years at Notre Dame. But in 1986, he was just the new coach. Reggie was a sophomore and walked into the football program's offices asking for a tryout. The secretary took one look at this tiny Hawaiian guy and got rid of him as fast as she could. But he kept going back. The coaches were always busy, so one time Reggie just decided to sit and wait.

Finally, one of the coaches came out and asked him what the heck he wanted. When he heard the kid say that he wanted to try out for the team, he told Reggie when tryouts would be for walk-ons or non-scholarship players. Reggie got his chance! But he didn't make the team. Most kids at this point would have said to themselves, "Well that's it, I tried." But not Reggie. Reggie started practicing. The only place he could practice at night was the parking lot by the stadium. It was a good place because it was well lit. He would practice and practice when he wasn't studying.

The next season he tried out again. Coach Holtz was surprised he was back and didn't want to turn the persistent kid down twice. So he thought it would be a nice story and let him on the team as a walk-on. Coach Holtz liked that he was quiet. He didn't want rabble-rouser kickers. The team already had a good kicker so nobody expected the smallest player on the team to ever play.

And that small player didn't play that season. He didn't mind not playing. The whole point of what he was doing was simply to be a well-rounded student. After games and practices, he would go to the library. He always had a mountain of studying to do. But in the 7th game of his 2nd season, Notre Dame was up 55 points to 13 and the coaches decided to let Reggie kick an extra point. He made it! He kicked it right down the middle. He was now in the record books. He had scored a point for his team. Reggie said that if nothing else ever happened for him on the football field, he had accomplished his goal and could die happy. He had done it. The whole team enjoyed it and it made everyone feel good. Coach Holtz thought that would be Reggie's only chance to ever kick.

The next season, Notre Dame's kicker had graduated and they didn't really have a kicker. Despite this, Coach Holtz said about Reggie, "Never did I think he would ever end up being our kicker, never in my wildest dreams." Leading up to the 1988 season, Reggie (and everyone else) kept thinking that a new kicker would step up. But nobody ever did, forcing Coach Holtz to rely on his tiny walk-on, med student kicker from Hawaii.

Lots of people thought this was the year that Notre Dame would be pretty good. They started the season ranked as the 13th best team in the country before playing any games. In the very first game of the season, they would play the #7 ranked team in the country, their rival...the Michigan Wolverines.

In the first quarter, Notre Dame's standout running back would score on an 81-yard punt return. Touchdown! Out came Reggie to kick the extra point. The TV announcers joked that he must have had to buy his jersey from the gift store because the team probably didn't have any small enough to fit him. He had done this once last season, but the coaches were probably pretty nervous that the moment would be too big for Reggie. It wasn't. He nailed it. Notre Dame 7, Michigan 0. Then a Notre Dame drive ends on the 14 yard line of Michigan. They have to kick a field goal. This would be the first time Reggie would try one of these but luckily it was only 13 yards further out than the extra point he had just kicked. This would be a 31-yard field goal. Reggie kicks it right down the middle! Notre Dame 10, Michigan still 0.

In the 2nd quarter, Notre Dame was still struggling to score on the Michigan defense. They send Reggie out yet again, this time for a 38-yard field goal. There was no need for the coaches to be nervous. All Reggie thought about was "I wanna make this kick!" He wasn't nervous at all. This was a nationally televised game. It was the most important game in the country that day. And none of that mattered to Reggie. He drilled it! Notre Dame was now up more comfortably, 13 to 0. But Michigan would score before halftime and again in the 3rd quarter to take the lead, 14-13.

With Notre Dame's offense still struggling, they send Reggie out a 3rd time. This would be an easier kick from 26 yards out. Reggie played it cool as a cucumber and sent his 3rd field goal right down the middle. Coach Holtz must have thought, "Man, we might really have something with this kid!" Notre Dame 16, Michigan 14. The Michigan kicker was really good and kicked a field goal from 49 yards out to regain the lead. Wow. Michigan 17, Notre Dame 16. The seconds were ticking off the clock and the game was nearly over. With just over one minute left to play, the Notre Dame offense stalled again. But they had gotten close enough for Reggie to have a chance to win the game. Now the pressure was really on! But after exhaling deeply, the smallest player on the team calmly drilled his 4th field goal of the day giving Notre Dame the victory.

The parties must have been fun that night on Notre Dame's campus in South Bend, Indiana. It was a massive victory. But Reggie would have no idea how the parties were. That's because he had to go to the library after the biggest game of his life and get back to studying. He was a senior medical student after all. And all that work paid off for Reggie. Notre Dame went undefeated that year and won a national championship. Without that win over Michigan, they likely would not have been in that championship game. Now he wasn't just in the Notre Dame record books. He would go down as a folk hero in the history of Fighting Irish football.

Reggie is now a cardiologist (a heart doctor) and he's a bit of a celebrity in the field of heart medicine. Lots of doctors show up to work with him having great respect for him as a doctor and having zero clue as to his sports heroics in 1988. Reggie is as humble as he's always been and credits hard work for everything he has achieved both on the field as well as professionally.

A Brother's Sacrifice

There was $14,000 on the line. That was BIG money in 1968. This was the very first time that the US Open, one of the major tennis tournaments in the world, would ever offer prize money to the grand winner. It was also the first time that professionals were allowed to play. But an amateur made it to the men's final to play a man they called the 'Flying Dutchman'. The two men were mired in a hard-fought, back-and-forth match. The amateur took the first set 14-12. Usually, a set is won by whoever gets to 6 points first but you have to win by two points. Because neither man could get a 2 point advantage, that first set went on and on. There wouldn't be a set in a major final that was longer than this one for another 30 years. Finally, the amateur won the 14th point ending the set. Next, the Flying Dutchman would battle back and win the 2nd set 7-5. It was now even. You had to win 3 sets to win the match. The amateur won the 3rd set 6-3. But the 4th set was won by the Flying Dutchman, 6-3. It would come down to the final set as the tiebreaker with both men having won 2.

In a military barracks, there was a man watching the match on television. He was at Camp Lejeune, the US Marine Corps base in North Carolina, and was getting ready to go back to the horrible war in Vietnam. But he was really happy to have the time to watch this tennis match. Another marine in the room wasn't used to seeing marines watch tennis but then it dawned on him. "Are you any kin to that guy?" The marine watching the match said, "Yeah, he's my brother."

1968 was the worst year of the Vietnam war. More soldiers died on both sides during that year than any other, including 17,000 Americans. And that marine, the brother of the amateur playing in the US Open... didn't have to be going back to war. He had chosen to. After serving one tour as a marine in Vietnam, he had signed up for another tour for one reason. There was a rule in the American military that they wouldn't send siblings into combat at the same time. Whole families had been wiped out in World War II and the military never wanted that to happen to American families ever again. He was going back to war so that his brother wouldn't have to.

That man watching in the marine barracks was sergeant Johnnie Ashe. He was watching his older brother, Arthur, play tennis on the biggest stage in the sport in peaceful Forest Hills, New York. Arthur was the amateur in that televised tennis tournament. Arthur was in the Army too, stationed at West Point Military Academy which was also in New York. Arthur was able to play tennis but had 15 months left of service which was plenty of time to get sent to Vietnam if Johnnie didn't go back. But Johnnie didn't want his gentle older brother to have to experience the war.

Johnnie signed up for the Marines when he was just 17. The war had already started. Johnnie knew he was signing up for war. Arthur was playing tennis in college at the time and leading his team to a national championship and winning a national championship as an individual. Oh, and the brothers were Black. There weren't many African Americans who played tennis back in the 1960s.

If Arthur won this final set he would be the first African American to win a major tennis tournament. That was a big deal in 1968. With Johnnie on the edge of his seat, it all came down to the final set. It was as back and forth as the rest of the match, but Arthur was unflappable. He was cool. He was calm. And he did what he usually did. With all that pressure on him, he outlasted his opponent and won the US Open. Arthur won the final set 6-3. Arthur was just a regular amateur, not a "registered amateur", so he wasn't eligible for the prize money. The $14,000 went to the guy he had just beaten. Today, the winner of this tournament gets $2.5 million. Arthur got $280. But none of that mattered to the two brothers. This was bigger than prize money. Johnnie was overwhelmed with emotion. With his fellow marines still jumping up and down, he quietly walked back to his bunk and pumped his fist as a surge of relief washed over him. His brother had done it.

Against the odds, Johnnie would survive his 2nd tour in Vietnam. He was left with deep emotional scars that torment soldiers who experience heavy combat. It didn't help that when he came back, he was spat on by war protesters. But he was proud of his brother and happy that Arthur never had to experience the war. Johnnie only told his father why he was going back to Vietnam. His dad would at some point tell Arthur the reason for Johnnie's 2nd tour.

Johnnie Ashe is a humble man. Arthur would go on to be a hugely important figure in the Civil Rights movement of the 60s and 70s. He would also be a great tennis champion winning many major tournaments and having an unbelievable career. Johnnie never wanted recognition for his sacrifice. He says "It's not really that important to me that they remember me. It was no big deal. We made sacrifices for each other in those days. I'd rather look at it as a footnote in Arthur's life than something miraculous that I did." But when Johnnie made that decision to go back, he knew it most likely meant his certain death. He had been lucky to survive his first tour of service in the war. He knew better than anyone that it would take a crazy amount of luck to survive a second one. He was willing to give his life to protect his brother. And that is a remarkable thing.

The Most Hit Batter in Baseball History and His Poor Skull

You've probably never heard of Hughie Jennings and I can't blame you. He played for 11 years as a professional baseball player. But that 11 years was all the way back in 1892-1903. It's been a while, but Hughie still holds one interesting record.

Hughie still has the professional record of being hit the most by a baseball while he's up at bat. What's the deal, did pitchers hate this guy? He was actually pretty well-liked. The answer lies in his fearlessness as a player.

Getting hit by pitches wasn't the only thing he was good at. He had one of the best seasons in baseball history for a shortstop in 1896, batting a crazy .401 batting average on 209 hits with 121 RBIs, and an insane 70 stolen bases. He was also one of the best defensive shortstops of his era. 1896 was also the season that he set the record for the number of times a player was hit by a pitch in a single season. He was plunked 51 times. Very rarely does anyone get hit more than 30 times in a season these days.

Hughie was hit an astounding total of 287 times during his 11-year career. Craig Biggio nearly beat his record by getting hit 285 times. Craig retired in 2007 and played for 8 more seasons than Hughie did, making Hughie's record an especially crazy one. Anthony Rizzo is the current player who has been hit the most with 178. He actually practices getting hit in the offseason.

In one game, Hughie was hit in the head in the 3rd inning. Batters didn't wear helmets in those days. He finished the game by playing another 6 innings and as soon as the game was over, he dropped to the ground unconscious. He didn't wake up for 3 days!

Maybe his toughness came from the way he grew up. As a young boy, he actually worked for a coal mine. How would you like to have grown up back then? Man those days were tough even for kids! And then there was the time when he was in college and he dove into a pool head first one night, not knowing that it had just been emptied of water. He fractured his skull that time and was lucky to live.

After his baseball career, he fractured his skull AGAIN! At least this time it wasn't in a swimming pool. It was in a really bad car accident. He also broke both legs and one of his arms. Ouch! Doctors weren't sure he would survive. But this is Hughie Jennings we're talking about, one of the toughest guys to ever play baseball, so of course, he survived.

Hughie became one of the best team managers or coaches after his playing days were over. He coached the Detroit Tigers to back-to-back World Series but they lost them both. He was known for his crazy antics as a manager. He would blow a whistle and shout and yell a lot. He yelled so much that he became known as

Ee-Yah Jennings. The crowds in Detroit loved it and would always cheer for him when he came out onto the field. He actually put himself in as a pinch hitter one time. The umpire asked him who he was hitting for and Hughie replied, "None of your business." Hughie was certainly one of baseball's most interesting (and toughest) characters.

The Guy Who Took 54 Years to Finish a Marathon

I have actually run a marathon before. Just one. And I was really slow. A marathon is 26 miles. That's an awfully long way to run. At least for me. It took me over 5 hours to do it. A ton of people in that same race ran it in less than half the time it took me. But I still beat a 1912 Japanese Olympian by 54 years, 8 months, and six days. Seriously?

Meet Shizo Kanakuri. He was the very first athlete from Japan to qualify for the Olympics. Think about that. He would be the first guy to represent Japan in Olympic history. That's some big-time pressure! The modern Olympics hadn't been around for very long in 1912. They had only had 4 previous Olympics. Yet, this was the first time someone from Japan would take part. Shizo was 20 years old and a year earlier had set the new world record for running the marathon. He ran it in 2 hours, 32 minutes, and 45 seconds. Many thought that he might be the fastest man in the world at that distance. He doesn't sound like the kind of guy who would take 54 years to run his next race.

He had aspirations for a gold medal. That would have been pretty amazing to not only be the first Olympian from your country but to win a gold medal as well. But this isn't that kind of story. The

1912 Olympics were held in Stockholm, Sweden. It was much harder to get from Japan to Sweden then than it is today. It's actually not so easy even today. It would still be a 10-hour flight. But that's a lot better than what Shizo had to endure. It took poor Shizo *18 days* to get there. That's an incredibly long trip. And to even make that trip, he had to raise the money himself. Not all countries paid to send athletes to the Olympics back then. Shizo's fellow college students and his older brother all raised the money for the trip. He would take a ship over to Russia and then ride the Trans Siberian railroad all the way across Asia. It was over 6,400 miles by train. I'm beginning to understand why Japan hadn't yet sent any athletes to the Olympics!

After that long trip, Shizo needed 5 days to rest before he could even start to train. And he probably didn't have the chance to run much during his super long train ride. To make matters even worse, the temperature in Stockholm that summer was above 90 degrees. This was much hotter than any of the runners had expected. I thought Sweden was supposed to be cold! None of this was looking very good for a medal marathon performance. After such an ordeal getting to the Olympics, it was finally time to race. But Shizo was already probably wishing that he had just stayed home.

He gave it his all out there on the course. Many runners were getting overheated and dropping out. Shizo made it 16 miles before he couldn't go any further. He was done. His exhausted legs refused to go any further. The marathon course at this Olympics took people out into the countryside. Shizo managed to make it to a farmhouse and a nice local family nursed him back to health. He would actually stay in touch with that family over the years. But nobody else knew what had happened to him. Shizo was really embarrassed about the whole thing. So many people had donated money to help the world record holder get there...and now this? He never checked back in with the race organizers so they had no idea what happened to him. As far as they were concerned, he had gone missing. And this was concerning because Shizo wasn't the only one who failed to finish the race. Only half of the 68 racers made it to the finish line and one runner from Portugal actually died from overheating.

The Swedish race officials must not have looked very hard for him. Shizo left Sweden in shame. Locals suggested that he might still be running around looking for the finish line. Four years later, the next Olympics were canceled because of World War I. Shizo would end up racing in two more Olympics. He finished 16th in the marathon at the 1920 Olympics in Belgium and raced again at the Olympics four years later but didn't finish that race either. But there were still some people in Sweden who wondered what had happened to him. Fifty years later, the missing Japanese marathoner had become a folk tale. A newspaper did a story about him making him more famous than anyone else who had been there in 1912.

The Swedish people have a pretty good sense of humor. And fortunately, so did Shizo. In 1967, he was finally tracked down and invited back to Sweden to finish his 1912 Olympic marathon. It was a big deal and captured the hearts of everyone who read about it. Lots of people came out for the race. It was all over the Swedish media and they had a ceremony for him and everything. When he finally crossed the finish line, Shizo was *76 years old*. It's a good thing he was still in such good shape! Over a loudspeaker, everyone heard an announcer say, "This concludes all the events from the 1912 Stockholm Games." Again... it was 1967. Everyone loved it when Shizo said that he managed to set another record by having 6 kids and 10 grandchildren while he was running a marathon.

Shizo lived to the age of 92 and remained active and in good health his whole life. He taught a lot of people about running and created a lot of races that are still run and quite popular. In Japan, he is still considered to be the "father of marathon." Shizo didn't let his failure in 1912 define the rest of his life. Even after he failed to finish that 1912 race and later set the record for the slowest marathon in racing history, he was still able to bring honor back to his name and left a legacy to be proud of.

That Time a Girl Struck Out Babe Ruth on 4 Pitches

Both the career and life of Babe Ruth were completely insane. I mean it. This guy was a complete freak of nature. He has had some of the most ridiculous records in baseball. I'll bet there's a lot you don't know about the player that was called the Great Bambino. That wasn't his only nickname. The Babe was even a nickname because his real name was George. He was also called the Sultan of Swat, the Colossus of Clout, the King of Crash, the Titan of Terror, the Big Bam, the King of Swing, the Wazir of Wham, Blunderbuss, the Wizard of Whack, the Prince of Pounders, the Mauling Menace, the Sachem of Slug, and on and on and on. That's a lot of nicknames! Babe was that good. But not always.

He certainly wasn't good growing up. He was a complete delinquent as a kid. He didn't go to school much. Instead, he just did whatever he felt like and ran all around the streets of Baltimore. He was finally considered "incorrigible" and sent to a Catholic school to shape up. The Babe did well there and it was there that he first learned about baseball. It might surprise you that he started his career as a pitcher. He wasn't just a pitcher, he was a star. He was one of the very best left-handed pitchers of his time. He had the

lowest earned run average and the highest winning percentage of any left-handed pitcher in the American League at the time. He even had one season as the best pitcher in all of baseball. He would go on to win 3 World Series games as a pitcher with a 0.87 ERA. The nearly 30 consecutive World Series innings that he pitched without allowing any runs was a record that lasted for 42 years.

The Babe finally talked his manager into letting him play in games when he wasn't pitching. After hitting home runs in 4 games in a row, he was now an everyday player. As well as being one of the best pitchers in World Series history, he would also become the best power hitter in World Series history with 15 home runs in only 167 at bats. That record still stands. The Babe played for years and years. Get this. His last 3 hits? They were all home runs! They happened in the *same game*. He was 40 years old and not the healthiest guy. When the Babe was 30, he collapsed on a train. He was so big that they couldn't carry him through the door. Doctors had to cut a hole in the train to get him out. Yet, despite not caring at all about living a healthy lifestyle, his final home run was the longest ever hit at the old Pittsburgh Forbes Field. In the 26 years that baseball had been played there, nobody had ever hit a ball over the right field roof. The Babe did, and that would be his final home run, number 714.

But despite taking the league by storm and being the most feared batter of his era, there was one pitcher that the Babe could never hit a home run off of. Actually, he didn't even get a hit. I'm talking about Jackie Mitchell, a 17-year-old girl. Four years before Babe Ruth retired, he was still very much in his prime. The Babe wasn't known as a big strikeout king. He did lead the league in strikeouts in five different seasons, but his strikeout numbers actually look really good to modern-day hitters. The Babe was actually pretty disciplined at the plate.

In 1931, the Yankees (Babe's team at the time) played in an exhibition game with the Chattanooga Lookouts. The Lookouts were a minor league team and are still around today. In 1931, Jackie Mitchell was the first woman to sign a major league baseball contract. During this exhibition game, the first two batters got on base. So the manager pulled that pitcher and put in Jackie to face the greatest hitter in baseball, the Great Bambino. You'd think this girl might be terrified. But she was as cool as a cucumber. She casually walked out there and threw a sinker ball. It was low so the Babe let it pass. But on the next swing, the Babe swung for the fences. He missed! Jackie threw again. Another Babe miss. He was a little grumpy by now. This was a girl throwing at him! So he ordered the umpire to inspect the baseball to make sure there wasn't any trickery going on. Jackie's next pitch was perfectly placed over the outside corner of the plate. Babe Ruth had struck out. The Babe was so repulsed that he threw his bat in anger. Next up was Lou Gehrig. Lou would tie Babe Ruth for home runs hit in 1931 and hit .341. The Babe and Lou were the heart of "murderer's row" which is what the Yankee's batting lineup was called because they were so good. But Lou swung and missed on 3 straight pitches!

Jackie would walk the next batter and get pulled from the game. The Yankees won 14-4. But they sure didn't score on Jackie. The next day, the sports section of the *New York Times* newspaper had the headline, "Girl Pitcher Fans Ruth and Gehrig". It was a big story and a fun one. Shortly after all of the press about Jackie had traveled across the country, her contract was ended by the baseball commissioner because "baseball was too strenuous for women." Some historians think that the Babe and Lou struck out on purpose. And most of those historians are men. Lots of others believe they were real strikeouts. The third baseman who was up next to face Jackie before she was pulled, said that he sure had no intention of striking out. As an old woman, Jackie said "(Heck), better hitters than them couldn't hit me. Why should they've been any different?" There's an awful lot that Babe Ruth got right during his wild and record-setting career. But on the second day of April in 1931...that was the day that a girl won one over the Sultan of Swat.

Great Play, You Caught
a Hot Dog Wrapper!

To be one of the worst fielders in baseball history, you have to be pretty bad. And you'd have to be able to handle getting yelled at by fans when you mess up. It would be really hard having tens of thousands of people watching you every time you make a mistake! Welcome to the life of the man known as "Dr. Strangleglove," "The Man with the Iron Glove," and "Stone Fingers."

I'm talking about the legendary Dick Stuart who started his career with the Pittsburgh Pirates in 1958. His career started off incredibly promising. His first hit was a home run! And even better than that, his second hit? A grand slam. Wow, who WAS this guy? To be such a terrible fielder and still have a baseball career, he had to be a pretty good batter. In his last season in the minors, he hit an incredible 66 home runs. The all-time record for a season at the time was Babe Ruth's 60. The brash Dick Stuart, just knew he would break that record and become the new home run king. I'm sure he especially thought he would accomplish that after his first two hits as a major league ball player. Of course, he also committed an error in his first game and that would be the beginning of Dick's true legacy.

Dick wasn't a bad fielder on purpose. He just didn't really care about fielding. He felt that all the glory was in hitting, so he never worked on his fielding. And without even attempting to get better at it...he didn't! Right from the start, he would lead the league for the next *SEVEN seasons in a row* in errors for first basemen. He was able to do that even though he actually started as an outfielder. Next, the Pirates tried him at 3rd base. But it usually doesn't work for teams to have such a terrible defensive player there. So pretty quickly he was moved to first base which was where teams used to put their worst fielders. These tended to be powerful hitters who weren't good enough fielders to be outfielders. Dick sure qualified for that.

He was also late to team meetings. Once, a manager was upset about this so he called a team meeting to discuss it. Dick was late to that meeting as well. When he walked in, he pranced down the center aisle like he was a fashion model and made everyone laugh, even the upset manager. But one of the funniest things about his career was the night in Pittsburgh when a hot dog wrapper was blowing in the wind. Dick saw it and grabbed it out of the air. 30,000 fans stood up and gave him a standing ovation for one of the best defensive plays of his career. When he was traded to the Boston Red Sox, he led the league in runs batted in. He hit the ball really well there. And because he played a lot, he set his own record for errors in a season with an astounding 29.

It was there in Boston that Dick quipped, "Behind every good man, is a woman." Notice, that he didn't say "good" woman? At that, a lady Red Sox fan yelled out, "If she is standing behind you, she better be wearing a first baseman's mitt!" Now that's a great line. Dick was really well-liked by his teammates, well... most of them. Some of the pitchers he played with probably weren't too crazy about all his errors. But he was well-liked because he had a good sense of humor about being such a bad fielder. He would even make lots of intentional errors in warm-ups to get a reaction from the fans. He was a real character. He hit some of the longest home runs in the league during his career. And he was the very first player in baseball history to hit 30 home runs in a season in both the National and the American leagues.

Interestingly, when Dick's streak of leading baseball's first basemen in errors finally ended was when his hitting started to go downhill. That season, he had 24 errors which is still a really big number. But his first team, the Pirates, had actually gotten themselves an even worse fielding first baseman than Dick. It was Donn Clendenon who beat him with 28 errors. I'm sure Pirates fans were thrilled to once again be forced to watch all of that terrible fielding at first base. Once he lost the crown of the worst fielding first baseman in the majors, Dick's career wouldn't last much longer.

That's what he was best at, after all. But he always had the one play he made on a hot dog wrapper...

The Remarkable Life of
One Cycling Frenchman

This story might be about the most impressive athlete in this entire book. You probably won't believe it. It took me a little bit to wrap my head around it. This is the completely spectacular story of Robert Marchand, who set a cycling world record...at *105 years old*.

That's right. This guy didn't even really start cycling until he was 67. When you read about his life, it seems as though it was simply because he was so busy seeing the world. But the root of it is that he was discouraged from cycling when he was young by a coach who told him that he was too short to be competitive. Oh, really? This is a great lesson. Most of the best athletes in history have someone in their past who didn't believe in them. Michael Jordan struggled to make his high school basketball team and got moved down to junior varsity. Stan Smith became the top-ranked tennis player in the world, but when he was young he couldn't even get a job as a ball boy because he was thought to be too clumsy. Tom Brady was truly the worst athlete in his entire NFL draft class. 198 players were picked before him to join the NFL. Few people thought he would make it in the pros. There are so many examples of this, I could go on and on. What matters is what YOU think. But back to Robert Marchand...

It's true that Robert was really short. He was barely 5 feet tall. He started racing on a bike he had put together when he was 14 and he won his very first race that same year. He joined a cycling club and raced a lot over the next few years. His coach told Robert that being so short would prevent him from ever being a cycling champion. That was back in 1930 when Robert was 19. He gave up his dream of cycling professionally. He became a firefighter instead. He did that for a long time.

During WWII in the early 1940s, he was thrown in a prison camp for his refusal to train the kids of people who were helping the Nazis. When he was released he was ready for a new adventure outside of France. He tried to go to Australia but they had closed their ports to new arrivals. So he chose Venezuela and worked there as a truck driver for eight years. But a dictator rose to power there so Robert headed north to Canada and became a lumberjack. This guy lived a really interesting life, didn't he? After years of lumberjacking, he moved back to France in the 1960s. But he didn't start cycling again until 1978 when he was 67 years old. He fell completely in love with it again. A few years later, he would peddle the 1880 miles from Paris to Moscow, Russia...as an 81-year-old. He raced in all kinds of really long races. He did a 372-mile race in 36 hours when he was 89. But he was still just getting warmed up. When Robert turned 100 years old, he was on his bike, of course! That year he would crash and have to go to a hospital. The doctors working that day were probably stunned by how old this guy was and how he got hurt. That crash didn't stop him. Weirdly, at 101 years old he was even faster than he was a year earlier. Then he started setting records for 62-mile races for cyclists over 100 years old. Then he set the record for cyclists over 105 years old! Amazingly, that was a separate age bracket. He biked the 62-mile race in 4 hours and 15 minutes. How'd you like to get beat by a 105-year-old? His time would beat almost all of us who aren't cyclists. After setting that record in front of a crowd chanting his name, he joked that "I'm now waiting for a rival."

Robert credited his health and ability to compete at such an incredibly old age to his healthy diet of vegetables and fruits, exercise, and going to bed at 9 o'clock every night. It probably helped that he was such a happy guy and always looked on the bright side. And why wouldn't he with all of his accomplishments? At 106 years old, his doctors reasonably asked him to stop trying to set world records. He did as they asked but didn't stop racing completely. He still did a 2.5-mile race that year. He liked to get out and bike with his (much younger) friends 4 times per week and always get at least one hour of peddling in every day. He died in 2021 at 109 years old. He was probably the fittest 100-plus-year-old person in the history of the world. The astounding and remarkable life of Robert Marchand proves that it's never too late to chase your dreams and become a champion.

The Most Dominant Athlete
in the History of Sports?

That's right. You're about to find out who the most dominant player in the history of sports is. Who do you think it might be? LeBron? Serena? Tom Brady or Tiger Woods? Those guys are all amazing and they're in the discussion for the best to ever play their sports. But as incredible as each of those champions are, they don't come anywhere close to matching the dominance of this guy.

This isn't one of the major sports like football or basketball. The ball goes 190 miles per hour. It's intense. And this champion is SO dominant...you won't believe it. His record is 619-55. Just to be clear, that's 619 wins compared to 55 losses. That's winning 92% of the time. And a lot of those losses were forfeits where he didn't even play or couldn't finish the game because he got injured. So his actual winning percentage is even higher! The last time someone really beat him? That was *NINE YEARS* ago. And that was his first non-forfeit loss in 4 years. That's *TWO* actual losses in the last 13 years. The next best player in his sport? He's beaten that guy 79 times and lost only 3. That's like LeBron being 82-3 against Kevin Durant. Or Tom Brady being 82-3 against Patrick Mahomes. It's insane. Okay, I've waited long enough. Who am I talking about?

I'm talking about Kane Waselenchuk, the racquetball player. Racquetball is a sport that is similar to tennis. But it's played in a cube-like room where you hit the ball off the wall. It's a lot of fun...unless you're playing Kane Waselenchuk. That second-best player I mentioned earlier? That's Rocky Carson and he's great. It's just that Kane is so much better. When Rocky isn't playing Kane, he's 592-157. That's pretty darn good. He's ranked as the 2nd best player in his sport. But even he is no match for Kane, winning just 3 times out of 82 cracks at him. Rocky talks about what that's like to be an athlete in a sport where one guy is so much better than everyone else. A lot of guys just give up and retire or quit the sport. Rocky says, "I've seen a lot of guys who don't have the heart to keep fighting. They're going onto the court thinking, 'Why am I even here?' or 'I wish I wasn't here.'"

Kane grew up in Edmonton, Canada. He grew up playing both racquetball and hockey. He started going to the racquetball club with his dad when he was just two years old. Just a few years later at 5 years old, he won a tournament. But he wasn't playing against kids his age, he was playing against grown women. They must have thought he was so cute before he beat them. In just another few years, he was eight and came in 2nd place at nationals in the division for kids under 10 years old. But he won in the doubles competition for kids under 14 years old...as an eight-year-old. He never had a coach, he just taught himself how to play. This meant he played differently than everyone else. He played racquetball like Spider-Man would, running up the wall to hit shots. He had to play that way because little kids aren't very tall. He went to Canadian senior nationals as soon as he could when he was sixteen. He says nobody knew about him. There were big-time professional players there, including the racquetball world champion.

Of course, that didn't matter to Kane. He was full of swagger and confidence. He even told the head coach for Team Canada that he would win the tournament. A 16-year-old? Hah! But this was Kane Waselenchuk we're talking about. He was no ordinary 16-year-old. He said he would win. And that's exactly what he did. There had never been a Canadian national champion so young. But every single racquetball record would soon be crushed. Kane had arrived. Sherman Greenfield was the reigning world champion at that tournament and Sherman made it to the finals just as he expected to do. The poor guy couldn't have known what was about to happen. This was when Kane put the racquetball world on notice. Sherman said that Kane had no weaknesses in his game. He could do anything he wanted to out there. And he knew it. Why else would a 16-year-old declare that he would win? About that crazy level of confidence, Sherman said "(Kane) probably has never had a thought that someone was better than him. That creates intimidation. You're out there playing hard and he's making it seem like you're in the backyard playground and he's on the pro tour."

Kane was also a really good hockey player. He was so good, that he was actually going to have a chance to try out for Edmonton's NHL team, the Oilers. But when he won Canada's National Racquetball Championship, he dove headlong into that sport giving up everything else. That's because he would start getting paid for the first time and it was good money. At 16, he would make $30,000 per year. He didn't pass up that chance. By 19, he had won that tournament another two times. That's when he moved to the United States to become a full-time professional. When he was 22, he finished the year for the first time, ranked as the top racquetball player...in the world. It sure didn't take him long. And remember, he still had never really been coached! When he was number 1, Kane decided it was finally time to hire a coach. Why? Because he wanted more. He knew that in order to stay at the top, he would have to keep getting better. So he called one of the best coaches, Jim Winterton. Jim asked Kane how good he thought he could be as a player. What do you think Kane said? "I don't know you that well and I don't want to come off as cocky or conceited, but I think I can be the greatest that ever played the game."

That's what Kane wanted. And that's exactly what he did. His success and complete dominance have been unlike any other athlete's in the history of sports. Even though his tournaments aren't on TV like other sports, what he has done is one of the most amazing things you could hope to find in sports. Kane is 40 now and still beating 22-year-olds. It doesn't seem like there will ever be another athlete as dominant as Kane Waselenchuk in racquetball...or anything else!

Potato Farmer in Rubber Boots Wins Ultramarathon

Marathons have runners traveling a distance of 26.2 miles. Anything more than that is considered an ultramarathon. These races are a test of athletic prowess, stamina, and focus. Many of these participants are highly trained athletes, who train and practice at high levels.

So what if I told you a 61-year-old potato farmer decided to run a 544-mile endurance race in Australia? You'd probably think that was pretty crazy and you might be right. But Clifford Young just liked running and so he decided to give the race a try.

He showed up on the day of the race in his overalls and rubber boots. I'm sure the other runners thought this was pretty strange running attire. He also didn't wear his dentures because he said that they rattled in his mouth when he ran. When the race started, Clifford took off at a slow pace. Throughout the day, a pretty sizable gap was established between Clifford and the rest of the runners. The other runners were pretty far ahead of him when they decided to sleep for the night.

Clifford did something pretty impressive. He just kept running. He didn't stop to sleep for 5 whole days! While the other athletes would stop for rest every night, Clifford would run. He eventually crossed the finish line first, winning the race by *ten hours*.

So how did he train for a race of this length requiring so much stamina? He chased his sheep. Being a farmer, Clifford was used to spending long days tending to and chasing after his animals. He told reporters that he had previously spent 2 or 3 days at a time chasing after his sheep. He even said that during the race, he pretended to be chasing after his sheep to round them up before a big storm. This motivated him to keep running.

The winner of the race was awarded $10,000 Australian dollars. But Clifford was astounded and said he didn't even know there was prize money for winning the race. He felt bad taking it from the other runners, who he said worked just as hard as he had. So he split the money with the five other runners who had finished the race after him. He didn't even take any for himself. What a nice guy!

The Australians loved Clifford's achievement so much that they set up a 6-day, 1,000-mile race that ran annually until 2005. He was awarded a Medal of the Order of Australia, an honor awarded to Australian Citizens for their accomplishments or great service. Clifford's story is a great reminder to find something you love to do and do it with all your heart!

Hear My Curse, for It Seals Your Doom!

One funny thing about sports is that it's full of superstitions. Sure, athletes can be really superstitious, but what about the fans? Fans can be even crazier than the athletes. One superstition is the curse. It's fun to come up with a reason why your team never wins. It probably feels better to be cursed than simply unlucky. Let's explore the most famous of sports curses.

Did you know that there is a legend about the Talladega Superspeedway in Alabama? They have a big NASCAR race there every year. They have all kinds of races there. According to legend, there was a Native American burial ground underneath it. Uh oh! That's never good. There are other rumors that a shaman cursed the whole valley that the racetrack is in when his tribe was forced out a hundred years earlier. In any case, the very first race at the track happened in 1969 and it did not go well. There was a problem with the surface of the track and most of the drivers quit in protest. Then there are the accidents. Everything from helicopter crashes to terrible car accidents in the parking lot, all lend credence to the legend of the curse. And of course, there were terrible accidents on the course itself. In 1973, driver Bobby Isaac, pulled over and quit during a race because he heard a voice telling him to. Creepy! It was probably wise for him to

listen. The next year, the top 10 cars in the upcoming race were found to have been sabotaged. It was done in a sophisticated way and nobody ever found out who did it, which led some to believe that it was ancient ghosts.

Can a video game be cursed? For a long time, it was believed that the NFL player who was put on the cover of the Madden NFL game by EA Sports every year, would be cursed. EA Sports comes out with a new version each year and puts the very best or most popular player on the cover of the game. The first version came out in 1988 and always had John Madden, the popular football coach and TV analyst on the cover. This never caused any issues for him. But in 1999 they started featuring players on the cover. The first was Garrison Hearst who had been breaking all kinds of records. In the playoffs that year he broke his ankle and was never the same player after that.

The next year they put Barry Sanders on the cover and he shockingly retired before the season! Then they released a version with Dorsey Levens on the cover after back-to-back Super Bowl trips. After being on the cover, poor Dorsey hurt his knee and was never the same player after that. The next year, it was Eddie George on the cover. Eddie had nearly won a Super Bowl the year before after an incredible season. And while he wasn't injured in his cover year, he was responsible for bobbling a pass that was intercepted which knocked his team out of the playoffs. The next season he was injured.

Talk of a curse started to pick up steam at this point. For the next decade, the great player put on the Madden cover would have their career end soon after. In 2010, for the first time, EA Sports put two players on the cover to try to break the curse. They chose two incredible players in Troy Polamalu and Larry Fitzgerald. Both players were injured but their careers weren't over, so maybe they were heading in the right direction? Lots of players would go on the cover and say they didn't believe in curses. But lots of them became believers after the misfortune that would happen to them during that cover season. Eventually, the curse was broken by Calvin Johnson who set the all-time NFL record for receiving yards during his cover season in 2013. Ever since that year, most players on the Madden cover have avoided injuries and terrible years. Rob Gronkowski and Patrick Mahomes would both win Super Bowls in their cover years of 2017 and 2020.

Other famous curses include the curse of the billy goat which haunted the Chicago Cubs for 71 years. The Cubs were playing in the 1945 World Series and a guy was kicked out of a game because he had brought in a goat with him. He said, upon being escorted out, "Them Cubs, they ain't gonna win no more." The Cubs would not play in another World Series until finally breaking the curse in 2016. Oh, and they lost that World Series in 1945 even though they were leading by two games when they kicked out the goat. According to his family, the goat owner sent the Cubs owner a telegram that read, "You are going to lose this World Series and you are never going to win another World Series again. You are never going to win a World Series again because you insulted my goat." There were countless attempts to "reverse the curse" that all failed. Apparently, Cubs fans just had to wait it out.

In Portugal, there is a soccer club called FC Benfica. They won five championships in only five years and had won back-to-back European Champions trophies. This was a really big deal and an incredible level of success. Their coach figured he was due for a pay raise. That seems reasonable. When he asked for the raise, he was either fired or denied. Pretty harsh in either case. He was really mad about it. Who wouldn't be? Most of us probably wouldn't have thought to utter a curse on the team though. But that's exactly what coach Bèla Guttmann did. He promised the owners that they would not win another championship for 100 years and stormed out. Bèla had won a total of 10 championships in his career and was really tough. He had even survived the Holocaust in a slave labor camp. He was tough and a great coach. Nobody is quite sure why he wasn't given a raise. But in the 60 years since his curse, FC Benfica has lost 11 chances at championships. Players have even gone to his grave and begged forgiveness. They may have to wait another 40 years!

The final two sports curses I'll mention were both cast by Romani Gypsies. And these Gypsies meant business. One of the oldest soccer clubs in the world is in Derby County, England. They were founded in 1884. In 1889, they built a new stadium where there was a Gypsy camp. They kicked out the Gypsies to start construction. This may not have been a great idea. The Gypsies said that the Derby County team would never win the FA cup. They were just laughed at because this was a really good team. But over the next few years, the Derby County Football Club would make the final four teams 6 times and play in the finals 3 times. But all they did was lose when it mattered, preventing them from winning the cup. They wouldn't play in another final until 1946, nearly 60 years after the curse. Descendants of the Gypsies were still around so a delegation was sent to ask them for forgiveness. With the score tied 1-1, the ball exploded. Everyone took this to mean that the curse was lifted and the Derby team won 4-1. The other time that these Romani Gypsies cast a curse is even spookier. It was a similar situation but in Birmingham, England. In 1906, the Birmingham City Football Club built a new stadium kicking out a group of Romani Gypsies from their camp. The Gypsies responded with a 100-year curse on the stadium. Eighty years later, one manager tried to beat the curse by peeing in all 4 corners of the field. It didn't work. On the exact 100-year anniversary, Birmingham FC won a game 2-1. Could this be a sign that it was finally over? And then four years later, they would win their first trophy in over 100 years by beating Arsenal in one of the most shocking upsets in the history of the League Cup Final.

The moral of this story isn't simply to avoid making Gypsies angry. There are countless other sports curse stories. They seem to come from our deep-seated silliness about such things. Humans tend to look for reasons where there may not be any. We want to know WHY do our beloved teams always seem to lose. We often need to believe that there is a reason for it and curses can be convenient reasons. But it is eerie when they play out just as the person who casts the original curse says they will. So who knows what is true? I won't pretend to.

"Dude, You Just Hit Your Dad!"

Rory McIlroy is one of golf's great champions. Even at a young age, he's had an incredible career. He's spent 100 weeks as the #1 golfer in the world and has won 4 major championship tournaments. He's *really* good. But this story is about a time when he wasn't so good.

It all happened at the 2021 Masters. The Masters is one of golf's major championships. Some would say it's #1. It is steeped in lots and lots of tradition. Unlike other major tournaments, it's always played on the same course in Augusta, Georgia. Whoever wins gets a green jacket. They've been doing that since 1949. The course opened in 1933 and the tournament is magical for golf fans. It represents everything that people love about the game. In some ways, it's the Super Bowl of golf. And it's the only major tournament that Rory hasn't won.

If a golfer wins all 4 major tournaments in their career, that's known as the Grand Slam. Only 5 golfers have ever won the Grand Slam. It's a short list that only includes Gene Sarazen, Ben Hogan, Gary Player, Jack Nicklaus, and Tiger Woods. Rory would love to make it on that list. But in 2021, things weren't looking good. Golfers go on streaks. It's a really hard game. Sometimes even the best players in the world feel like they can't hit anything. It takes a ton of work to get good, and a ton of work to stay good.

2021 was Rory's 7th try at the Grand Slam. If he can just get that green jacket! It was the first day of the 4-day tournament. He was on the 7th hole and already 2 over par. That's not terrible. But Rory had been struggling in recent tournaments with his swing. So much so that he had hired a new swing coach.

The 7th hole at the Masters is 450 yards. That's 4 and a half football fields. Rory hit a decent drive to get started but the ball had bounced behind a tree. He was hoping to hit his next shot up on the green to have a try at a birdie which would take a point off of his score. In golf, you win with the lowest score, unlike most sports. Rory swings. Uh oh. His club face was just a smidge too open and he pushed the ball a bit too far to the right. "Fore!" That's what you yell when you hit your ball towards other people and they need to watch out. His ball was heading right for the spectators watching him play. Yikes! Did it hit someone? It sure did. It bounced off a poor guy's leg. Ouch! It really hurts getting hit by a golf ball.

But that was no ordinary spectator that he hit. It was his own dad! What are the odds of that? Not only did he hit his dad, but his dad was the guy who got Rory into golf and coached him all of those years. Rory's father's name is Gerry. And it was Gerry that gave Rory his first golf club when Rory was only 4 years old. He showed Rory how to grip the club he had given him and they probably took some practice swings with it. Little Rory took it to bed that night and even held it with the proper grip as he fell asleep. He would beg his dad to take him golfing all the time, nearly every day. Rory loved it.

He became the youngest member of their country club golf course when he was only 7 years old. He showed a lot of promise. Rory's mom, Rosie, worked every shift she could at a factory so that they could afford the money it cost to play golf and to hire coaches. Gerry also worked all he could to support Rory. He actually worked two jobs to help Rory get good at the game. And they were dirty jobs. One was cleaning toilets at a rugby club during the day and then he would go and work at the golf course at night. Rory's parents were always working. And they were doing it for Rory. (Their hard work and sacrifice really paid off as their son is now worth more than $170 million dollars.) But now this? Of all people to hit with a golf ball!

When he got hit, Gerry joked, "I should get an autograph!" People actually get hit by professional golfers every now and then. Usually, when that happens, the golfer will give them an autographed glove and maybe even a little money as a way to be nice. When reporters told Rory about his dad's joke, he said, "He's seen me sign plenty of stuff over the years, so I think that's the least of his worries. I think he just needs to go and put some ice on. Maybe I'll autograph a bag of frozen peas for him."

Rory wouldn't make the cut that year at the Masters. That means his score wasn't good enough after two days to keep playing the final two days. So Rory is still looking for that Grand Slam. Maybe this is the year? I know one thing. Gerry will probably be extra careful if he goes to watch!

Watch Out for Those Ducks!

Henry Robert Pearce, also known as Bobby Pearce, was an Australian rower who won Olympic gold medals in 1928 and again in 1932. But he came very close to losing one of the quarter-final races in 1928. How, you ask? A family of ducks was crossing the river in front of his boat, and Bobby, being a gentleman, waited for them to cross. Here's the scoop!

Bobby was the third generation in his family to compete in the sport of rowing. When Bobby competed, he rowed in the event for single scullers. A sculler is when the rower uses two oars. Bobby would sit in a small, narrow boat, facing backward with an oar on each side of the boat. The rowers, or scullers, use the oars to pull and propel themselves through the water.

In 1928, Bobby was considered an amateur rower, but he was the only rower from Australia who qualified to compete in the Olympic Games. Bobby headed to Amsterdam to compete and even got to carry his country's flag. With his likable personality, he was instantly popular with the locals and rowing fans. In early races, he beat his two competitors by an unprecedented time of nearly 30 seconds each.

Then came the quarterfinals. Pierce was up against the Frenchman Vincent Saurin, who would go on in his career to win nine national titles and medals at three different European championships. In other words, he was no slouch.

The race began and Bobby took an easy lead. He was gliding through the water when he started hearing a ruckus on shore. The crowd on the bank of Sloten Canal was yelling and pointing at something in front of him. Remember, Bobby is facing backward in his boat. He turns to see what all the fuss is about and sees a mama duck, with a family of small, fluffy, yellow ducklings crossing the canal directly in his path. Bobby, with his big heart leading the way, pulled up and stopped his oars, leaning on them until the ducks were safely out of his way.

The problem was that Bobby's opponent didn't have the same regard for the duck family that Bobby did. Vincent Saurin used the opportunity to not only catch up to him but to gain a five-boat-length lead before Bobby was able to get back in the race. Luckily, Bobby proved again to be a much more powerful rower and he was able to regain his lead and even won by almost 30 seconds!

Bobby would go on to win the gold medal in that Olympic games as well as the hearts of the people of Amsterdam. His win would set a new world record that was 25 seconds faster than the previous record. He was also awarded the Philadelphia Gold Cup, presented to the amateur champion of the world. Bobby's story is a tale that proves that being the nice guy certainly doesn't mean you have to finish last!

The Champion Wrestler
With Only One Leg

Anthony Robles knows a thing or two about learning how to play to his strengths. He was born with a disability that could have kept him from realizing his dreams, but instead, he learned to use his disability as an advantage.

Anthony was born with only one leg. Doctors didn't have an explanation, as he was otherwise a healthy baby boy. But one of the legs just wasn't there, it stopped just below his hip.

Doctors would create a prosthetic leg for young Anthony, but he hated wearing it, saying it pinched and was uncomfortable. Instead, he became skilled at getting around on crutches and that became his preferred method of mobility.

As you can imagine, Anthony was not super excited about going to school. Having only one leg made him a little insecure, which is understandable. But when he was 14, he found a way to change all of that.

Anthony started going to watch his older cousin's high school wrestling practice. He was fascinated and the coach asked him if he'd like to give it a try. His cousin encouraged him to join the team. Anthony was instantly hooked, but he wasn't very good. Not yet, anyway.

In his freshman year, he had a record of 5 wins and 8 losses and was ranked last in his city of Mesa, Arizona. But his coaches kept encouraging him and

Anthony decided to look at how he could play up to his strengths. Sure, he only had one leg. But he had incredible upper body strength. When he was only in 6th grade, he beat the school record for the most push-ups in the whole school. Getting around on crutches made his upper body strong. He kept working and with the help of his coaches, he began to improve. He used his low center of gravity as a defense and even created some new offensive moves.

By his junior year, Anthony was on fire. He finished out his junior and senior years with 96 wins and 0 losses. He won two state championships. By the end of his senior year, Anthony, who had once been ranked last in his city, became a national champion.

Even with his incredible record, he ended up not being recruited by the colleges he was most interested in attending. He decided to stay close to his home and went to school and wrestled for Arizona State University. Much like his high school career, it took him a little time to find his groove. But by his final year of wrestling, he ended the year with 36 wins, 0 losses, and was a 3-time conference champion. He also added the title of NCAA national champion to his stats, along with being voted the tournament's most outstanding wrestler.

After college, Anthony decided to use his love of wrestling to motivate people and made a career out of helping others realize their potential. He is passionate about using his experiences to encourage others to be unstoppable, too.

The Jockey That Came Back to Life

Horse people are dedicated. Horses are big and they take a lot of work. The riders willingly get on 1,200-pound animals and ride them around. Jockey Ralph Neves took that dedication to a whole new level. During a race track accident, Ralph fell and was declared dead by medical professionals. But did he let that stop him? Of course not! He came back from the dead and was clamoring to ride in the next race. Here is his tale.

Ralph grew up in California where he learned to ride horses. As a kid, he dropped out of school and became a movie stunt double. I'll bet a lot of you reading this would sign up for that deal in a heartbeat! A stunt double performs some of the more dangerous activities for the actors in movies. He found his sweet spot performing as a stunt double while riding horses. He could make $10 a day being a stunt double but was paid $50 every time he was asked to fall off a horse. He once made $200 in a day because he was asked to fall off four times!

Ralph was a competitive guy and he soon found a way that he could combine his competitiveness and his horse skills...horse *racing*. At 18 years old, Ralph started winning races and he never looked back. Local newspapers were quoted saying that when he got on a racehorse, failure never seemed to enter his mind. He was fearless and never minded taking a chance, even if he put himself in danger doing it.

He had an aggressive racing style that sometimes got him in trouble. Track officials gave him several suspensions for being too hard on the horses and making too many risky, dangerous moves. But Ralph just kept riding the only way he knew how...going for the win.

In 1936, Bing Crosby, a famous singer and actor, issued a challenge to the jockeys at the Bay Meadow track. The winner of the most races for the multi-day meet would receive $500 and a gold watch. Ralph lived for this sort of challenge and met it head-on. On the first day of the meet, he was in first place. He wanted that prize!

The next day, he had an early race on a horse named Flanakins. He took the lead early, but in the last part of the race, Flanakins stumbled, the motion throwing Ralph to the ground. Unfortunately, he couldn't get out of the way of the rest of the horses surging up the track behind him and Ralph was trampled.

Ralph was loaded into the back of a pickup truck and taken to the track infirmary. He did not have a pulse. Track doctors were not optimistic but they gave him a shot of adrenaline and had him sent to the hospital.

The findings at the hospital were not any better. Doctors couldn't find a pulse, so they declared him dead and sent him to the morgue. Back at the track, the announcer called for a moment of silence to honor jockey Ralph Neves, who had passed away.

But Ralph still had races to win! In a miraculous recovery, Ralph regained consciousness. He woke up wearing his ripped riding pants, one boot, and a toe tag with his morgue identification number. I'm guessing the people at the morgue were pretty shocked to see him walk out of there and hail a cab back to the racetrack.

Back at the track, jockeys in the locker room thought they were seeing a ghost. Nope. It was just Ralph, trying to get back to winning races! He argued with track officials that he felt fine and could still complete his races for the day, but the officials were unwilling to take that risk and refused to let him ride.

He was back at it the next day and although he didn't win any races, he had enough 2nd and 3rd place finishes to make up for it and he ended up winning Bing Crosby's challenge. The $500, the gold watch, and all the glory was his. He just had to cheat death to do it.

Ralph was a jockey for 30 years, continuing to push the boundaries and take risks. He had several other injuries including a broken back and emergency brain surgery. He rode 25,334 horses, won 3,772 races, and won over 13 million dollars. He won the George Woolf Memorial Jockey Award for his contributions to the sport of horse racing. He died for the second time in his sleep, at the age of 79.

C'mon Now, Do People Really Do That?

There are some fascinatingly bizarre sports in the world that you've probably never heard of. And I think it's great when people get creative and have fun. But these sports are much crazier than hot dog eating. I'm all for hot dog eating as a sport, I just mention it because it gets covered on ESPN these days while the sports I'm about to tell you about don't.

Let's start with one of my new favorites. Chess boxing. What? Seriously? Yes! This is real and it's as awesome as it sounds. And there are actually *two* governing bodies of the sport! There's the World Chess Boxing Organisation based out of Berlin, Germany, and the World Chessboxing Association in London. The contestants alternate rounds between boxing and chess. The way you win is either with a knockout or a checkmate. You fight for a round of three minutes and then play chess for four minutes. There's a big tournament in London and clubs all over like the Los Angeles Chessboxing Club. There's a lot of strategy involved. If you're a better fighter than you are a chess player, you try to delay during the chess portion and get aggressive in the boxing ring. The opposite is true if you're a stronger chess player than you are a fighter. But you'd better be able to take and

throw a punch if you get into this sport. There are former UFC fighters working with chess coaches that have become passionate about chessboxing. There's something really cool about seeing people play chess shirtless, inside a boxing ring. It's also interesting that the sport was invented by a comic book artist and took off from there.

Next up is a sport that you may find a bit more boring but whoever irons your clothes may find it more exciting. Let me introduce you to the Extreme Ironing Bureau. They basically just add ironing clothes to every extreme sport they can think of. Participants actually iron a shirt while they are skydiving, paddleboarding, rock climbing, deep-sea diving, bungee jumping, and on and on. Basically, it's about getting to an extremely difficult to get to location with a battery-powered iron and ironing board. It was started by a guy whose brother would iron his clothes even when he was out camping in a tent. The Extreme Ironing World Championships take place in Germany every year. And there was strangely a break-off group from extreme ironing that started doing extreme vacuuming. Okay, now we're just getting carried away with this!

Have you ever gone kayaking? It's a fun pastime that involves paddling a little boat that is smaller than a canoe. This wasn't exciting enough for some kayakers though and giant pumpkin kayaking was born. Let me tell you about the Windsor Pumpkin Regatta in Canada. To win, you can't paddle a kayak. You have to get your hands on a giant pumpkin, hollow it out...and paddle that to victory. The Canadian race was the first but now you'll find this fun craziness in Wisconsin and Vermont as well.

Those last few "sports" are much newer. This one has amazingly been going on since the 15th century. It's cheese rolling. My bet is you've done something similar to this, just without the cheese. You know how fun it is to roll down a hill right? Well...on Cooper's Hill in Brockworth, England, they simply give a big roll of cheese a one-second head start, and then chase it down a *REALLY* steep hill. People come from all over the world for this. It's impossible to actually catch the cheese, it picks up too much speed. It usually goes over 70 miles an hour. (A while ago the cheese was replaced by a foam wheel) Once, the cheese crashed into a spectator. I'll bet that hurt! Whoever crosses the finish line first, wins. But Cooper's Hill is so steep that most people don't stay on their feet. They just somersault wildly down the hill. Lots of injuries happen. But there's no paperwork involved, anybody can just show up to the hill and give it a shot during the once-a-year event.

Here's a sport that's even older and sounds really difficult but fun. Camel Jumping. It's ancient. In Yemen, there are guys who do it as their job! They're professional camel jumpers. Yemen is a desert country so they have plenty of camels. It's like the long jump but over camels. The goal is to try and jump over as many camels as you can. This is usually done at special events like weddings and festivals. You've got to be an awfully good athlete to jump over just one camel, much less three or four like the pros can.

This would be a really long book if I only focused on all of the lesser-known sports in the world that have competitions. So I'll just mention a few more that I think you'll find interesting. There's also underwater hockey, shin kicking tournaments, lawn mower racing, toe wrestling tournaments, pillow fight leagues, bubble football, wife carrying (a race in Finland where men run carrying their wife), and organized snowball fighting. And there's SO MUCH more. The world is a crazy place filled with fun, crazy people with big imaginations who love to compete at just about *anything*!

The (Almost) Perfect Game

You shimmy to the edge of the lane and eyeball the ten white pins that are standing 60 feet straight ahead. You draw back that big shiny ball in your hand, let it swing forward, and release it. The ball flies down the lane, hooks at just the right time, and swings in to hit the very center pin. All the pins come tumbling down with a loud thwack. STRIKE! You just made the ultimate bowling move!

A strike is when you knock down all the bowling pins in one hit. Now imagine you do that twelve times in a row. Pretty impressive, right? It sounds hard. And it is. Even professional bowlers struggle to score the perfect game.

Even harder than scoring the perfect game is scoring the perfect series. A series is three games played in a row. In order to score a perfect series, you would need to get a strike 36 times in a row. Wow!

Bill Fong loves the game of bowling. In January of 2010, Bill headed to one of his favorite bowling alleys, the Plano Super Bowl in Plano, Texas. His bowling league met there every Monday night to bowl together. Little did they know that something extraordinary was about to happen.

That night his team, the Crazy Eights, drew lanes 27 and 28. Coincidentally, these are two of Bill's favorite lanes. Lane 27 hooks a bit while lane 28 is more of a direct straight approach.

Yes, Bill takes extensive notes on his bowling. He knows how the lanes in each bowling alley roll. He makes notes on any variances he notices throughout his bowling game so he can tweak his performance and make better moves. It's what helps a good player become great. And on this night, Bill's attention to detail would serve him well.

As his teammates started rolling their balls down the lane, Bill noticed that they all seemed to hook just a touch too early. They would miss that opportunity for getting the strike that all bowlers crave. So Bill made adjustments to his roll, took a touch deeper spot, and was rewarded by knocking down all ten pins. He was off to a good start.

The game went well, with Bill able to focus and adjust his game as necessary. Four strikes in a row felt good. The fifth roll made Bill hold his breath. The number ten pin didn't go down right away. It teetered and wobbled before another pin knocked into it, sending it to its fate. Whew! Another strike.

The game went along with Bill getting strike after strike. At the end of the game, he had done it. He had rolled the perfect game! Twelve strikes in a row for a score of 300. His name was announced over the loudspeaker for his accomplishment.

On league night, Bill's league bowls what is known in bowling as a series. That's three games in a row. So Bill had two games left to bowl. What he did next made a lot of bowlers turn their heads and take notice. Bill changed the ball he was using.

Bill remembered from previous bowling nights, that these two lanes changed a little as the night went on. The way the ball approached the pins altered and so Bill modified his game, too. Many of his friends thought he was crazy to mess with a good thing (he just rolled a perfect game), but Bill trusted his instincts.

The strikes kept coming. One after another in the second game, Bill continued to roll strikes. There was something magic in the air. Bowlers from other leagues took notice when it was Bill's turn. Everyone stayed out of his way and tried to keep quiet. No one wanted to mess up a streak like that.

And so it happened. Bill rolled a second perfect game. This was getting crazy. Back to back 300 games, 24 strikes in a row. He was on fire! His name was again announced over the loudspeaker and everyone came over to congratulate him.

But Bill still had one more game to finish and he was ready to get down to business. As he watched the balls roll down their assigned lanes, Bill again decided to change balls.

His risky move was again rewarded with strike after strike in his last game of the night. By the sixth frame, Bill had acquired quite the crowd around him. His friends said they were more nervous than he was. Each time he would pick up his ball for his turn, the crowd would go silent, watching the ball roll down the glossy floor. And each time the ball would make contact and send all ten pins to the ground, the crowd would erupt into cheers and applause.

In the tenth frame, something happened. Bill began to get nervous for the first time. Could he do it? Could he actually roll the perfect game? The enormity of what was happening finally hit him and nerves took over. As he released the ball, he knew immediately that it wasn't on the right track. He watched it hit and all except for pin number nine toppled neatly over. The nine pin stood there, taunting him until another pin rolled in its direction making it tumble to the ground. A close call, but still another strike. Only two more to go.

As Bill walked back he began to feel dizzy and very sweaty. But he got himself together to roll another strike for his 35th strike in a row. Now he was down to the final roll.

The ball left his hand for his 36th roll of the night and it looked just the same as every other perfect shot he had taken. Traveling down the path with the same precision as each previous shot, it looked like the perfect roll. But then the unimaginable happened. That darn number ten pin refused to topple. It refused to fall down. It wobbled precariously but stayed standing.

His friends, who had been prepared to erupt in celebration, instead grabbed him to hold him in this moment of defeat. How could it end like this? Thirty-five perfect rolls and one pesky pin ended Bill's hope of scoring the extremely elusive perfect series.

A perfect series is a score of 900. Bill had a score of 899. Still an incredible feat, for sure. With this score, he beat the Texas state record. And at the time of Bill's score of 899, only 11 other people had ever accomplished that. And only 15 people had ever bowled a perfect game of 900. Think about that. Out of all the bowlers in bowling alleys every day all over the world, there have only ever been 15 perfect series and even fewer scores of 899. Bill was amongst spectacular company.

Later that night, after celebrating with friends, Bill went home and began to feel sick. He was dizzy and sweating and sick to his stomach. He ended up in the hospital the next day where doctors informed him that he had suffered a stroke. They said it was very likely that during the game when he experienced feeling nervous and dizzy, it could have been the first in a series of small strokes. Bill was very lucky to be alive. He ended up having open-heart surgery and was told he only had a 30 percent chance of surviving. But Bill had beat other incredible odds, and he survived the surgery. He had a bowling league to get back to!

Bill still bowls and although he hasn't yet bowled his perfect 900 game, he has scored several times in the 800s. He says for the perfect game, all the stars have to align. And he still hopes one day it will happen for him.

Giving New Meaning to the Word "Touchdown!"

Michael Strahan is one of those guys that everybody loves. He started his career as a professional football player and even won a Super Bowl. Then he transitioned into a television career, where he won two Emmy awards. This progressed into being a co-anchor for the morning news show Good Morning America. But in December of 2021, Michael added another notch to his resume as...astronaut.

That's right! The record-setting football player launched in a spacecraft, setting another new record as the tallest person to ever fly in space.

Michael got his start as a football player in the NFL for the New York Giants. It took a few years for his career to really take off, but he found his groove. He was named Defensive Player of the Year and set a new record for the number of sacks in a single season. He played professional football for 15 years and in 2008 helped the Giants win the Super Bowl. He was inducted into the Pro Football Hall of Fame.

Two years later, Michael got asked to be a guest host on the morning talk show, *Live With Regis and Kelly*. The fans loved him so much that when Regis decided to retire, the network asked Michael to stay. They changed the name of the show to *Live with Kelly and Michael*. Ratings went crazy. Together with his co-host Kelly, Michael won two daytime Emmy awards for "Outstanding Talk Show Host." He was so popular that the network ABC asked him to join as a full-time broadcaster for *Good Morning America*.

While working for *Good Morning America*, Michael got an offer he couldn't refuse...to go up in space! The aerospace company, Blue Origin, is making it possible for humans to travel to space as tourists, even if they aren't actually well-trained astronauts. For promotional coverage, they offered Michael the opportunity of a lifetime, a ride into space on their spacecraft, the New Shepherd.

The spacecraft was named after Alan Shepherd, the first U.S. astronaut. It is reusable, meaning it can launch and land multiple times with very few alterations, making it environmentally friendly. The journey lasts eleven minutes, where the passengers have the opportunity to experience the incredible views of our earth from the windows of a spacecraft. The craft takes off and climbs 3 times the speed of sound. Passengers experience several minutes of weightlessness before beginning a careful parachute descent back to the landing zone.

Michael was one of six people to take this launch into space. His flight was the spacecraft's third passenger space flight. Michael and one other passenger were honorary guests meaning they didn't pay for their seats, but the other guests were paying passengers. They probably didn't mind Michael being there because he's so much fun to be around. Although he is such a big guy, it was probably just a little crowded.

So, how much would you pay for a trip into space? There is a lot of speculation about how much seats cost and there doesn't seem to be any set price. Some people seem to have paid between $200,000 and $400,000 for seats. One guy paid $28 MILLION! One thing is for sure, space travel is going to have to get a little bit cheaper for me to afford it!

So what did Michael say about his space experience? In interviews, he mentioned how transformational it was, even just preparing for the journey. The danger involved in a moment like that gave him a new perspective on how much his friends and family meant to him as he prepared for this adventure. Seeing the earth and experiencing weightlessness was an unbelievable experience. It was very moving.

From Super Bowl champion to an award-winning talk show host to an astronaut...Michael Strahan proves that you really can be anything you want to be!

Want to Avoid War? Send in the Globetrotters!

The late 1950s were a scary time for a lot of people. That's because everyone was afraid of a nuclear war. World War 3 was looming as a real possibility. This was the era of the Cold War. That's a pretty weird name for a war, isn't it? A "hot war" was considered one where armies were shooting at each other. So a cold war was one where there were countries that did not like each other and the relationship was so tense that it could turn into a hot war at any time. What could war have to do with the Harlem Globetrotters? Do you know about the Harlem Globetrotters? Let me tell you all about them.

First of all, they've always been the most beloved and liked basketball players on the planet. Why? Not only are they amazing players, but they're funny and entertaining to watch. They have been delighting audiences and making them laugh for nearly 100 years now. Their uniforms are dazzling red, white, and blue. But what they can do with a basketball is even more dazzling. At one time, they were easily the most famous basketball team in the United States and always drew the biggest crowds to their games. Their origins start all the way back in 1926. They even had their own cartoon for a while. People loved them because they

showed incredible skill with the basketball and were so funny about it. Never before had anyone taken a sport and made a comedy show out of it. The Harlem Globetrotters were really unique and special.

The man behind the team was Abe Saperstein. He was part basketball man, part circus promoter and he helped the Harlem Globetrotters become world-famous. The Harlem Globetrotters were made up entirely of Black players. In the 1940s, the NBA didn't have Black players. The best team in the NBA agreed to play the Globetrotters in 1948 thanks to Abe's persistence. This was a big deal, seeing the Globetrotters beat the Minnesota Lakers. It was a close game, but the Globetrotters hit a game-winning shot at the buzzer. Just two years later, the NBA would open up to Black players. That Globetrotters win had a lot to do with it.

In 1958, Wilt Chamberlain joined the Globetrotters. He could have gone into the NBA but he chose the Globetrotters instead. He would move on to the NBA a year later and become the most dominant player in the entire history of the league. Wilt was over 7 feet tall. He was one of the most amazing basketball players of all time. It was during Wilt's year with the team that something amazing happened. Abe Saperstein had been trying to get permission for the Globetrotters to do a tour in the Soviet Union in Moscow, Russia. He thought it was important and that his team could help the relationship between the United States and the Soviet Union. He had been working on it for 10 years. But because the two countries hated each other, this had always looked like it might not happen. The countries kept looking more and more like they would be entering into a full-blown war. So when the Harlem Globetrotters, in their USA flag-style uniforms, finally got permission from the United States government to go to Moscow and play 9 games for Russian audiences, it was just in the nick of time.

When they got there, the Globetrotters found Moscow to be a very cold place. The KGB, the secretive Soviet police agency, followed them everywhere they went. They were told not to say anything controversial, and not to go sightseeing anywhere by themselves. Even for the fun-loving Globetrotters, this was a serious trip. It was serious not only because the situation between the two countries was serious, but the Russian people were very serious! During the first Globetrotters show, before a packed audience, nobody laughed. This was very different from a usual Globetrotters show. American audiences laughed and had fun. But the Russian people didn't believe in showing emotion in public places. They were more serious people than Americans were. There were 14,000 people watching the show, but it was completely quiet. So the Globetrotters changed up their strategy. Meadowlark Lemon decided to just start running around slapping hands with the audience. The Globetrotters were all about having fun, but this was something the Russian audiences didn't seem to grasp. Eventually, the entertaining Globetrotters began to win over the Russians. Humor translates across any culture and any language.

The Harlem Globetrotters ended up being a smashing success in Moscow. They met the country's leader, Nikita Khrushchev, and that went well. The Globetrotters' performances showed the people of the Soviet Union that people everywhere are really all the same. When people realize this fact, it's harder to want war. Who could want to fight these funny, fun-loving American basketball players and showmen? It was impossible to watch the Harlem Globetrotters perform and not like them. They turned out to be the best goodwill representatives that the USA could have possibly sent in that tense situation. They definitely played a small role in helping to prevent World War 3. They have gone on to perform in 123 countries over their history, spreading joy and goodwill everywhere they go. Joy and peace go hand in hand. And the Harlem Globetrotters have been a symbol of that for nearly 100 years.

Foul Ball!

Have you ever caught a foul ball? If so, you're really lucky. The odds of catching a foul ball are about 1 in 600, so the chances are not great. Here is the story of a lady who caught not just one but TWO foul balls. But she didn't think it was so lucky...

Alice Roth was the wife of the sports editor for *The Philadelphia Bulletin* and an avid baseball fan. She loved the Phillies and would regularly attend games with her husband and grandsons. She was in attendance at the game on August 17th, 1957, a day that Alice and her grandsons would remember years later.

She was sitting in the stands along the third base side when Hall of Fame player Richie Ashburn came up to bat. Richie was known for being a fighter on the mound and making pitchers work. He swung the bat and hit a foul ball up into the stands.

Poor Alice was in the wrong place at the wrong time. The ball hit her directly in her face, breaking her nose. Blood was everywhere! Medics showed up to usher Alice out of the stands and to the hospital. They got a stretcher and were taking her towards an exit when the unthinkable happened.

Richie Ashburn was still up at bat. The pitcher threw the ball. Richie swung the bat and hit another foul ball. The ball flew through the air and made direct contact with Alice AGAIN! This time it hit her in the leg and broke a bone in her knee. Luckily medics got her out of there before she got hit a third time!

Alice was taken to the hospital where she eventually made a complete recovery. Richie Ashburn came and visited her in the hospital several times. He autographed a baseball for her and even sent her Christmas cards every year.

The next time Alice and her family went to see the Phillies they were given the royal treatment. They got to get there early to watch batting practice and watched the game from the press box. One of her grandsons asked Alice if she could go to an Eagle's game and get hit in the face with the football! Alice said her grandsons got the benefits and she got the broken nose. I guess if you're going to get hit with a foul ball, you hope that you've got a good story to go along with it!

The Swimmer Who Saved 20 People From Drowning

Shavarsh Karapetyan set 11 world records and won 17 world championship titles in fin swimming. But that's not what made him a hero in Russia and Armenia. He's a hero because he didn't mind jumping into a dangerous situation when needed, even if it meant putting his own life at risk.

Shavarsh had a knack for finding himself in situations where he had to think fast and act quickly. On three separate occasions, he would find himself facing a perilous situation. He always chose to act with courage and bravery.

Shavarsh was born in Armenia. He learned to swim at an early age and soon took up the sport of fin swimming, in which the swimmer races using fins to propel themselves through the water. This type of swimming tests an athlete's endurance and strength. Shavarsh trained hard, running for miles every day, and practicing breathing techniques.

His first dangerous encounter happened in 1974, while he was riding in a bus traveling to a sports center. The bus broke down and the driver got out to see what the problem was. However, he forgot to set the parking brake. The bus began to roll backward, towards a gorge that was located just off the road behind them.

Shavarsh acted fast, pushed past everyone on the bus, hopped into the driver's seat, and yanked the parking brake which stopped the bus just in time. I'll bet that got his adrenaline going. That was a close one!

The next time Shavarsh had to hurl himself into danger came in 1976. He and his brother had gone out for a run. To train, Shavarsh would often run 12-18 miles with a 45-pound sandbag in his backpack. That's quite the athletic achievement just doing that! He had completed 12 miles when suddenly it sounded like a bomb had gone off. He looked around and saw that a trolleybus had veered off the road and was now sinking in a lake. As the trolleybus began to sink, Shavarsh did the one thing he was best in the world at doing. He dove into the water and started swimming. He broke the back window of the submerged bus by kicking it in with his foot. He got a large cut on his leg, but he didn't feel the pain. His focus was on saving as many of the 92 drowning passengers as possible.

Shavarsh kept pulling people out of the bus and swimming them to shore where other rescuers were pulling them to land. He would dive again, returning to the bus for more people. He pulled 37 passengers out of the bus and 20 of those people survived. Finally, rescue workers had to tell Shavarsh to stop as he was so exhausted that they feared for his own safety. Those people owed their lives to the lucky coincidence that one of the best swimmers in the world happened to be on a trail right where they crashed.

Unfortunately, the cut on his leg became infected and his lungs suffered from the cold, polluted water. He ended up with blood poisoning and pneumonia, which landed him in the hospital for 45 days. His recovery was long and hard. Once he was well again, he found that he could not swim as easily as he had been able to before the accident. He struggled with breathing and found that he did not enjoy the water anymore. He competed for the last time in 1978, before retiring for good. Even after the accident, he was able to win gold and bronze medals at the European Championships and set new records for his events. At his retirement, Shavarsh had won 17 world championships, 13 European Championships, 7 Soviet Union Champion titles, and set 11 world records.

Even with his heroic act, not many people knew the story of Shavrash Karapetyan. His government refused to allow newspapers or reporters to print the story. The government didn't want people to think that it was normal for trolleybuses to crash and wind up in lakes. His deed went mostly unnoticed until 1982. A reporter working on a story on fin swimming heard about it and wrote a careful article highlighting Shavarsh's bravery. He became an instant hero in the Soviet Union, receiving thousands of admiring letters and being awarded a Soviet distinction, an Order of the Badge of Honor.

Amazingly, in 1985 Shavarsh's courage would be tested a third time. This time he happened to be in an area where a building caught on fire. Shavarsh did what he did best, act as a superhero. He rushed into the burning building to help save people that were trapped inside. He was badly burned and again spent a long time in the hospital.

Shavarsh now leads a mostly quiet life. He lives in Moscow where he started his own company designing and selling shoes. He got the opportunity to carry the Olympic torch for the opening of the 2014 winter Olympics, demonstrating that his courage and bravery were appreciated and he was well respected by the people of his country.

Runner Wins Gold by...Riding in a Car?

The 1904 Olympics were the first Olympics held on American soil. One event in particular, the popular marathon, was such an incredible fiasco that it's a wonder that the United States was ever allowed to host the Olympics again. The bizarre events that took place during the marathon sound like something that may have been acted out in a comedy show, but this really happened.

The 1904 Olympics coincided with the World's Fair, both of which were held in St. Louis, Missouri. As you can imagine, having these two big events within the same year had planners and officials working hard to make sure that everything was perfect.

The Olympic organizer tasked with designing the marathon course was James Sullivan. He wanted to build a course that would truly challenge the athletes, pushing them to the brink to maximize their skills and athletic prowess. And he did exactly that. The course is said to be one of the most challenging marathon courses ever. It was even slightly shorter than a traditional marathon, measuring in at only 24.8 miles, versus the standard 26.2 miles. But that didn't matter.

The runners were a bit of a rag-tag group who added plenty of character to the story. Several of the

Americans were well-known runners and marathon winners, but Fred Lorz was a bricklayer by day and did all of his training at night. The Greeks sent along 10 men who had never run a marathon before. Two men from the Tswana people of South Africa decided to race and showed up at the marathon with no shoes on their feet. Interestingly, these two men were the very first African athletes to compete in an Olympics.

One was called "Len Tau" by race officials because they couldn't pronounce his actual name, Len Taunyane. The other was Jan Mashiani. They would finish in 9th and 12th place but Len Taunyane would have done better had he not been chased a mile off course by wild dogs. This was one crazy race.

Another interesting tale is that of Andarin Carvajal, a Cuban mailman who arrived in New Orleans eager for his Olympic chance. But he lost all of his money at a game of dice and had to walk to St. Louis. That's 700 miles! He arrived at the starting line wearing his pants, a long shirt, and a beret. An Olympic official found a pair of scissors and helped to fashion a pair of shorts by cutting his pants off at the knee.

The race started at 3 pm on a terribly hot day. It was 92 degrees when they fired the starting pistol. The runners took off, ready to tackle the challenging course...or so they thought.

The roads back then were not paved, and this course seemed to be on the dustiest roads possible. Wagons and automobiles were on the roads in front of the runners, kicking up generous amounts of dust.

An American, William Garcia began coughing so hard from the dust that he ripped his stomach lining and had to be hospitalized. Another man became sick from heat exhaustion and decided to quit.

The race course went through incredibly difficult terrain. Not only was it over dusty roads, it also went through parts of town. This meant that the runners had to dodge traffic, trains, trolley cars, and automobiles. It was one of the hilliest courses ever designed. Seven huge hills had the runners trekking up and down, over and over again. One official said the course was, "the most difficult a human being was ever asked to run over."

The course designer was also a believer that dehydration allowed athletes to be able to obtain their peak performance, so he allowed only one water station in the whole 24.8-mile course. The dehydrated athletes were begging for water. Thomas Hicks, an American favorite, became so weak that his trainers mixed a concoction to help him continue to press on. Back then, performance-enhancing drugs weren't illegal. Thomas' coaches mixed egg whites and strychnine (also known as rat poison!) This was believed to give a person a shot of energy, but it didn't really do the trick for poor Thomas. Within another few miles, he was bleary-eyed and stiff, and his coaches had to give him another mixture of the concoction.

Cuban runner Andarìn Carvajal, who had walked from Louisiana, snatched two peaches from surprised spectators and ate them as he ran. He later passed an apple orchard where he enjoyed a snack of apples. Unfortunately, Andarìn chose rotten apples and later had to stop running because of severe stomach cramps. He decided to take a nap on the side of the road. He would eventually finish just out of the medals in 4th place.

Way up the road, near the finish line, spectators cheered as they saw a runner approach. "An American!" the crowd cheered. Fred Lorz, the American bricklayer, crossed the finish line and was about to have the medal hung on his neck when officials began to protest. It turns out that Fred had completed 11 miles of the race by riding in a car! The cheers turned to jeers as the angry crowd booed Fred. He claimed he had never planned to accept the medal but really did it as a joke. (Fred would go on to win the Boston Marathon the next year, this time choosing to run instead of riding in a car.)

After the debacle with Fred, another American was spotted near the finish line. Thomas Hicks, loaded up on egg whites and strychnine, was coming into view. However, he was so exhausted (and I'll bet the strychnine wasn't helping) that he began to hallucinate. He believed the finish line was still 20 miles away and he begged for a nap. His coaches refused, pushing him forward and finally, propping him against their arms, they helped move his shuffling feet over the finish line to be declared the winner.

Of the 32 runners who started the race, only 14 finished. The winning time of 3 hours, 28 minutes, and 45 seconds is still the slowest time ever recorded in Olympic marathon history, a whole 30 minutes slower than the next slowest time. This proves what a strenuous and demanding course the runners set out to race that day.

I think the main lesson of the story is that if you are going to race in a marathon, make sure a crazy person didn't design the course. Oh, and you should probably stay away from dice games too to avoid the whole "walking 700 miles to get to a marathon race" thing.

Jocko Flocko, NASCAR's Monkey Co-Driver

NASCAR has a colorful history full of crazy and interesting characters. One of them is Tim Flock. He's in the NASCAR Hall of Fame. Another of those interesting characters was Tim's co-driver, Jocko Flocko. Tim came from a racing family. His sister, Ethel, was the 2nd woman to race in a NASCAR race, and his two brothers, Bob and Fonty Flock, also raced. The very first NASCAR season was held in 1949. All 3 Flock brothers, or the "Flying Flocks" as they were known, finished the season in the top 10 of the points standings. That's a pretty impressive family accomplishment!

Tim was the youngest of all his siblings and was the last to start racing. But in 1952, the 4th year of NASCAR's existence, he won 8 out of 34 races. That winning percentage made it one of the best seasons in NASCAR history. Tim actually finished his career with a winning percentage that has never been beaten in the seventy-plus years since NASCAR started. He won 40 times in 189 races. In the 1952 season, it came down to one final race. All Tim had to do was to start the race and he would be the season's champion, but he wanted to win. He raced in his typical daredevil style and hit a wall and flipped the car. Tim later joked that

"I bet I'm the only guy who ever won a championship while on his head."

After the best season of his life, and as the new NASCAR champion, things got...weird. It was now 1953. Tim was off to a bad start that season. Tim's manager happened to walk through an Atlanta pet store and saw what he thought might give Tim a boost. It was a monkey named Jocko. Tim's manager sure had some funny ideas! He thought that it might distract the other drivers, seeing a monkey in one of the cars. And they could name the monkey Jocko Flocko which he thought had a catchy ring to it.

But Tim, as you might imagine, wasn't so sure about this idea. For one thing, it was against the rules to have a passenger with you during a race. He was eventually talked into it, he just wouldn't mention it to NASCAR. His team made Jocko his own uniform with a helmet and harness and a monkey-sized seat to keep him safe. In Jocko's first race, they were winning the race for 87 out of the 150 laps but finished fourth. Not bad for a monkey. After the race, Tim introduced Jocko to all the fans. Suddenly, Jocko Flocko was a star.

NASCAR didn't seem to mind their first co-driver and in the next few races Tim and Jocko finished in sixth place, fifth place, and then they had a 2nd place finish. They were getting better and better together. Or maybe Tim was just getting used to racing with a monkey in the car. In their next race, they would make history.

It was May 16, 1953. They were in Hickory, North Carolina, at the Hickory Speedway. This was a dirt race track where they would go 200 laps for a total of 100 miles. They won! Jocko Flocko was now officially, the fastest monkey in the world. He's still the only co-winner or even co-driver in all of NASCAR history. This would be Tim's only win of the 1953 season after dominating the year earlier. Maybe it's because he couldn't keep racing with Jocko...

Unfortunately, the racing career of Jocko Flocko would not last much longer. Two weeks after their historic win together, the pair found themselves at a brand new racetrack in Raleigh, North Carolina. It was paved and the oval course was a mile long. This was the very first Raleigh 300. The drivers (and Jocko) would race 300 laps. The drivers were over halfway done and Tim and Jocko Flocko were still in championship form. They were in 2nd place only behind Tim's brother, Fonty Flock. (This story is full of fun names.) And that's when disaster struck. Jocko escaped! He was loose in the car and there was nothing Tim could do about it.

There was a hole in the floor of the car that Tim could open by pulling on a chain. This was so that he could see how his right tire was doing. As soon as Jocko Flocko was loose, he stuck his head down the hole. Tim explained what happened next. "We had this chain hooked onto the floorboard that we would pull up to check on the wear on the right front tire. Well, old Jocko had been watching me do that, and soon as he came unstrapped he went right for the hole and stuck his head through. The tire zipped him on the head, and he liked to have went crazy."

Poor Jocko Flocko went crazy. Now, Tim was not only in a NASCAR race with a loose monkey in the car with him...but an angry loose monkey in the car! Jocko Flocko was hopping all over the inside of the car and would even scratch at Tim. Tim had no choice but to pull into a pit stop to get Jocko Flocko out of the car. This allowed Fonty to win the race and Tim finished in 3rd place despite the unscheduled pit stop. Tim knew that he couldn't bring Jocko Flocko with him anymore.

Maybe Jocko didn't like being strapped inside a race car. Or maybe he would have been okay if hadn't stuck his head through the hole in the floor. In any case, Tim decided that it was probably best if NASCAR drivers didn't race with animals in their cars.

Tim wouldn't win another race that year without Jocko. He even got his head run over by a car while napping before one of the races later that season! Lucky for Tim, he only got a concussion. The fans loved Jocko Flocko and so did Tim. So it was sad that he couldn't race anymore but it sure was fun and crazy while it lasted!

Mush!

Perhaps you've heard about the famous dog sled race held annually in Alaska? The Iditarod Trail is a grueling course that runs for 938 miles from Anchorage to Nome. Every year in March, the top sled dogs and their mushers gather to see who can complete this demanding test of skill, resilience, and training. The winner receives ultimate bragging rights and a cash prize.

The Iditarod Trail wasn't always about who came in first place or who was the best musher (dog sled driver.) The first race on the Iditarod Trail was actually a life and death situation.

The town of Nome, Alaska was remote, meaning it was pretty hard to reach. It was nearly 1000 miles from the bigger city of Anchorage, and those were not an easy 1000 miles. Alaskan wilderness covered the distance between the two towns, making the residents of Nome often feel very isolated from the rest of the world.

In 1925, the children of Nome began to get sick with a terrible cough. The town doctor realized that it was diphtheria, a serious infection that makes breathing and swallowing painful and difficult. Everyone in town (but especially the children) was in danger. A quarantine was put in place, but without an antitoxin serum, the effort would most likely be useless.

The nearest antitoxin was in Anchorage, but with the Alaskan winter wilderness looming between the two towns, it couldn't have seemed further away. The harbors were frozen, making boat travel impossible. The winter air was too cold for airplanes to safely fly. Even the nearest train station was 700 miles away, in Nenava.

The 1,400 people living in Nome were in a real pickle. The governor of the area decided the best option was to have a relay team of sled dogs carry the vital serum to the town of Nome. At this time, the mail carrier service used sled dogs for mail deliveries. A team of the very best sled dogs and mushers was put together. Some raced ahead to their designated checkpoints to await the important arrival of the medicine.

On the evening of January 27, 1925, a train arrived in Nenava transporting the extremely important cargo. The package was wrapped in fur and handed to "Wild Bill" Shannon. At his signal, his nine dogs and sled were off on the first of this incredible and important journey.

Over the Alaskan tundra, with temperatures reaching sixty degrees below zero, this was a test of stamina and mental strength. The majority of the sections of the trip were broken into 30-mile sections, with one musher handing off the precious package to the next waiting team at a designated meeting point.

The last leg of the trip was Gunnar Kaasen and his team of dogs led by sled dog, Balto. By this point, the crew would find themselves in a blizzard. Balto had to rely on scent, rather than sight, to stick to the trail. At one point a wind gust flipped the sled, sending the package of serum into a snowbank. Luckily, Gunnar was able to dig and find the unharmed package.

In the wee hours of the morning on February 2nd, Balto led a yipping and excited sled dog team down Front Street in Nome, Alaska to deliver the vital supplies to the town doctor. Over the next few days, the antitoxin was given to the town residents and within three weeks the quarantine was lifted. The town could go back to normal.

This heroic sled journey utilized over 150 dogs and 20 men. They completed the route in five and a half days, which was half the time it usually took and that was through a blizzard! Years would go by without much attention to the Iditarod Trail's history, but in 1967, Dorothy G. Page was working on Alaska's centennial celebration and wanted to use the Iditarod trail as a way to honor the past and heritage of Alaska. The idea of the Iditarod Trail Sled Dog Race was born and over the years has evolved into an annual affair with mushers from all over the world. Most years about fifty mushers and one thousand dogs show up to participate. The nearly 1000-mile journey includes 26 mandatory checkpoints and the mushers are obligated to take three rest stops of varying lengths. Before the race even starts, mushers fly in supplies to these checkpoints with food and essentials for the care of their dogs.

Although the trail has changed very little from the first running of the Iditarod in 1973, the time it takes to complete it sure has. In 1973, the journey took a little over 20 days. In 2021, a new record was set with a completion time of 7 days and 14 hours. Those sled dogs must be moving fast!

The Iditarod Trail really embodies the spirit of Alaska and has become an event that is known around the world. And to think it all started with a group of brave mushers and sled dogs trying to save the children of Nome.

The Inner City Kids Polo Team That Became Champions

The sport of polo is sometimes called the sport of kings. Often associated with wealth and prestige, this sport requires a team of riders and horses, usually expensive equipment, and skill and precision on horseback. So how did a bunch of inner-city kids come to dominate the sport?

In 1994, Leslie Hiner started a program to help kids from the rough parts of Philadelphia, Pennsylvania. Kids were getting in trouble at school, being disrespectful, and heading for a lot of trouble. These areas of the city had a history of fighting and violence that started young, even with kids who were in school. These kids didn't always get positive guidance at home and needed somebody to show them a good path to follow. This is where Leslie was able to step up. She started a small horseback riding stable and allowed 20 kids to come learn how to ride and care for horses. The catch? The kids had to help do chores and take care of the barn. They also had to uphold the high standard that Leslie expected.

The program was called Work to Ride and kids were asked to write a 300-word essay in order to join the program. Leslie didn't really care what they wrote. She cared that they put in the time and effort to complete the task. Horses are hard work and they take a lot of commitment.

The kids in the program are required to uphold a certain set of rules. This means not only helping with horse chores, but each student has to keep their grades at a C or above. Leslie helps tutor any kid that is struggling in school. She also has a no swearing policy and makes the kids work together to solve problems.

In the beginning, the kids learned horsemanship and how to ride. But their stable area was small and they were getting kind of bored with riding in circles in the arena. That's when Leslie, who had been playing polo as a hobby, introduced the kids to the sport. They watched a fast-paced match, with quick horses performing nimble moves, and became hooked. There were sticks, balls, and goals and it seemed exciting and intense. It was kind of like hockey but on horses.

The kids loved it. Leslie said they were willing to work hard because they were so interested in learning how to play polo. So they set out to learn the basics. Polo is played in a big open field. Leslie would have to put the horses in the trailer to take the kids and horses to the polo field. They showed up looking a little out of place. The wealthier players had nice equipment and fancy horses, while the Work to Ride kids had mismatched, hand-me-down equipment, and ordinary horses.

Leslie made them feel like they belonged though, and slowly the team got better. It took five years, but they finally won a game. After that, everyone on the team seemed to become more confident. The kids realized that their talent and hard work were getting them exactly what they wanted, so they kept at it and kept improving. Now they were showing up at events, still with mismatched equipment and ordinary horses, but they were competing...and WINNING!

There weren't too many high school-level polo teams to compete against. So in order to practice, the Work to Ride team often played against elite Ivy league Universities like Cornell and Harvard. Work to Ride would be the college teams' warm-up game opponent before they played their "real" competition. Kareem Rosser, who was team captain when he played said, "I guess it's funny because I think we're supposed to lose, so it's kind of funny that we'd end up winning or we'd end up with a close game."

Seventeen years after the Work to Ride program started, they experienced one of their ultimate victories. The team won the Interscholastic National Championships and became the first African American team in history to win a polo championship.

The Work to Ride program is still going strong. One success story is Kareem Rosser, who graduated from high school and attended Colorado State University where he played polo and won the collegiate polo national championship. In 2016 he was voted Intercollegiate Polo Player of the Year. He graduated college and works in finance now, but he still helps support the Work to Ride program.

Learning how to dream big and how to work hard to make those dreams come true is what the Work to Ride program is all about. Many kids that have gone through the program have gone on to have very successful lives, in spite of being raised in an area of town that is known for its violence and hardship. And their amazing polo team is a force to be reckoned with!

Making History,
One Skatepark at a Time

They're called the X Games. And each year, 100,000 fans show up to cheer on their favorite competitors as they perform gravity-defying flips, achieve maximum air, and attempt daredevil stunts. There's a lot of speculation as to why they are called The X Games. The most likely reason is that it was started as a way to appeal to extreme sports enthusiasts from Generation X. The X also stands for eXtreme sports, something that this event highlights. There is also the element that in mathematics, X usually stands for the unknown...and The X Games is full of athletes pushing the limits into the unknown.

Skateboarding is always a highlight at The X Games. Fast and fun to watch, the skaters get out on the ramp and have a time limit to show off their moves, trying to impress judges and land new tricks. Brighton Zeuner didn't set out to make history in skateboarding. That just happened naturally, kinda like how she fell in love with the sport. Brighton used to tag along to the skatepark with her older brother. She would play on the sides and watch, until one day her parents got her a skateboard of her own. She messed around with it and found out that she really liked it. It gave her a feeling of freedom and made her push herself to try new things. Plus, it was just a fun thing to do with her brother and dad.

It turns out that Brighton was pretty good though. Her family moved to California and decided to build a big skate ramp in their backyard. This helped her get better and showcase her talent. She started competing and winning at age nine. She was even beating her brother, who luckily was a good sport about it. "She's kind of a natural. I wasn't. I didn't really care," her brother, Jack, said. Brighton says that there are some street skating moves that he excels in and he has taken over filming her skating. Do you think your sibling would be as easy going as Jack?

In 2016, Brighton made history when she became the youngest person ever to compete in The X Games where she came in fourth place. She was just 11 years old! Later on that year she would compete and WIN the Vans Park Series Championship that was held in Sweden. Her career was just getting started.

The skateboard park event is what Brighton excels at. The park event gives each skater a 45-second time limit to show off all their skills. They skate around an enclosure with ramps and obstacles, crafting flips, jumps, and launching themselves off the side. "Think of it like a dance routine," Brighton says. A panel of judges scores each skater's session and the highest score (usually with the craftiest, most exciting moves) wins. Brighton likes that you can make up your own ways to do different tricks. She likes the creativity involved in skateboard park and that there aren't specific rules on how to do things. Each skater has their own creativity and style.

In 2017, (one day after she turned 13) Brighton became the youngest person to win a gold medal championship at The X Games. She said the feeling was crazy, but she was just still a normal 13-year-old kid. She just happened to be an exceptional skater.

In 2018 she did it again, making her the youngest competitor to win back-to-back X Games championships. She even made the team for the 2021 summer Olympics in Beijing. Here she made history again, as this was the first time skateboarding was offered as an Olympic sport.

Being an Olympic athlete at only 17 years old may sound a little daunting, but Brighton just loves to skate. "I didn't even mean to be serious with it. It just happened naturally. That's why I love it," she said. She practices for hours every day, opening up her backyard skatepark to help other local skaters. Sometimes Tony Hawk, a professional skater and video game star, will pop in to skate for a while. Brighton has gotten the chance to skate and learn from some of the best. They all say her fun-loving attitude and ability to handle pressure make her a great skater.

At the end of the day, Brighton is just another kid who likes to express her imagination in different ways. She hopes to use her influence as a skateboarder to help grow other creative outlets in her life. She loves to write songs and stories, design clothes, and play guitar. Brighton's story is a reminder to everyone to pursue what makes you happy.

The Power of a Coach

Having a coach or a mentor who believes in you is often the key influence on people that are successful. Having someone believe in you is a very powerful motivator. People tend to work harder and put in more effort when someone is there to encourage them along the way.

You don't have to tell that to the Summerville, South Carolina boys basketball team. They met their coach and motivator when they were in eighth grade, and he told them that when they were seniors in high school, they were going to win the state championship. That's a pretty powerful prediction. And these boys needed somebody to believe in them. That somebody was Coach Louis Mulkey. Basketball was his passion and he loved to help kids learn to play the game. He was the captain of Engine 15 for the Charleston Fire Department, but if he wasn't at work you could find him helping kids improve their skills.

When he met the boys in their eighth-grade year, he told them that he had confidence that they were going to be GOOD. So good, in fact, that he believed they could win the state championship in their senior year. Coach Mulkey was the kind of coach that helped his players on and off the court. He made sure that his players always had a good meal before their games, sometimes picking one of them up and buying them dinner. He would occasionally loan them money if they needed it. And he was always there, with advice, encouragement, and incredible basketball coaching skills. Many of the players said Coach Mulkey was like another father figure to them.

With Coach Mulkey's guidance, the team trained hard. They improved, winning games and getting better every season. Finally, it was the summer of their senior year, the year when it was all supposed to come together for them.

Coach Mulkey was at work for the fire station on June 18, 2007, when a call came in that a local furniture store was on fire. His crew responded quickly, but the blaze was massive. Smoke from the fire went on for miles. While he was working to try and contain the fire, Coach Mulkey got separated and lost from his crew. When his emergency radio call came in, it was too late for the crew to find him. Over the radio, his last words were, "Tell my wife I said I love you."

The fire ended up being the biggest firefighter tragedy since September 11, with a total of nine firefighters losing their lives that day. The whole town was devastated, but the basketball team took it especially hard. When they gathered for practice at the start of the school year, they made the decision to train and play as hard as they could to honor their coach... and friend.

The Charleston Fire Department had a memorial black fire helmet made with the number 15 and Coach Mulkey's name engraved on the side and presented it to the team. At the start of the season, that fire hat was on the bench, placed in the fourth seat, in the spot where their beloved coach had sat every game. That helmet would go to every game to remind the team who they were playing for.

The Summerville boys basketball team had an outstanding season, heading into the playoffs with 20 wins and only 3 losses. But could they keep it up? The boys won three straight playoff games which led them to the semifinals. It was a close game, with a tight score through most of the game. Near the end, the Summerville fans got into the spirit of the situation and started a chant to rally the players. "Lou-is! Mul-key!" echoed through the basketball gym that night as the Summerville players pulled off an amazing win. They were heading for the state championship game!

This game wouldn't be an easy one. Quick baskets had the lead jumping from one team to the other, always within a few points of each other. The boys were playing their hearts out, with their coach's helmet sitting on the bench motivating them to make his prediction 4 years ago a reality. More than anything, this team wanted to win that State Championship to honor their coach and thank him for his confidence in them, both on and off the court.

It came down to the final few seconds of the game. Bruce Hanes scored a 2-point shot for Summerville, putting them in the lead. This could be it. There were only 1.2 seconds left on the clock when the other team's player rebounded the ball and threw a miracle shot 65 feet through the air towards the basket. The buzzer sounded. The ball had swished through the net.

Defeat. They had come so close to winning that game. But wait! The referees got together to discuss the timing of the last shot. They talk in hushed tones on the sidelines. The crowd waited, holding their breath for the final call.

The final shot by the opposing team was overruled. The buzzer had sounded before the ball had left the player's hand. The Summerville crowd went wild! They had their victory. Lauren Mulkey, the wife of Coach Louis Mulkey, joined the team on the court to celebrate the championship that they had won for her husband.

There was one final stop on the way home from that triumphant night. The boys stopped at the grave of their coach. The boys said a prayer, thanking him for his guidance, support, and unrelenting faith in them. A few of the boys even left their state championship medals at his grave.

This story is a powerful testament to the power that encouragement can have in a person's life. Find someone who motivates and inspires you, and then work hard to be that inspiration for others.

King of Big Air

Have you ever fallen off your bike? It hurts, doesn't it? Maybe you scraped your knee or elbow, or perhaps even broke a bone. Riding a bike is mostly safe, but it does come with a few risks, especially if you like to try tricks and stunts on your bike.

Mat Hoffman is no stranger to bike wrecks. In fact, he has broken over 60 bones, been knocked unconscious over 100 times, and nearly died once. I know what you're thinking, "Man, this guy must be really bad at riding a bike!" It's actually the opposite. Mat rides BMX bikes and is considered one of the best in the sport's history. Due to his dedication to biking and performing daredevil stunts, Mat is credited with developing modern-day BMX as we know it.

So what is BMX? It stands for bicycle motocross and it's an extreme cycling sport. There are two main divisions for the sport. In BMX racing, riders race their bikes along dirt tracks with hills and obstacles. In freestyle BMX, the riders perform tricks and jump in front of judges to see who has the best moves. Mat really enjoys freestyle BMX.

Mat grew up like a lot of kids, riding his bike around his street and in his backyard in Oklahoma. He was the youngest kid of four, so he was used to watching his older siblings try new things and he wanted to do everything, too. His dad built a ramp for his bike in their backyard and Mat started playing around with different tricks. He loved to use the ramp to get his bike completely in the air so he could add different moves while he was airborne.

BMX biking wasn't a super well-known sport at the time. It wasn't like Mat had a coach or a training facility to teach him and help him get better. He was just a kid living his dream in his backyard. He decided to enter his first BMX competition at Madison Square Gardens. When he got there, he was the only rider wearing a full-face helmet and body armor. It soon became apparent why. Mat said he watched the other riders and realized he was going way higher than anybody else. This self-taught kid from Oklahoma was only 11 years old!

Just a few years later, Mat went to a competition where he won the amateur division. An hour later, he decided to turn pro and rode in the professional division of the same competition. He won that, too. Being a professional allowed him to earn money for winning competitions and he could also get sponsors. EVERYONE wanted to sponsor him. Mat took professional riding to a new level. He was going higher than all the other pros, inventing new tricks in between every competition, and pushing the envelope to what was normal. It was clear that he had a very special talent.

So how did Mat learn all these new tricks? He practiced. And he fell A LOT! He learned that thrift stores would throw away old mattresses so he would go and pick a bunch of them up to try and cushion his falls. Sometimes it worked, sometimes it didn't!

Once, while he was riding at a competition, he tried a new trick that had never been done before, now called a flair. It's a combination of a backflip and a 180 turn. Mat knew he had someone special in the audience. A kid from the Make-A-Wish Foundation had come to watch his performance that day. After the ride, Mat gave him his bike. Super cool move!

During this time, most of the bike ramps were 8-10 feet high, so riders would be launched about another 8-10 feet into the air. Mat decided that it wasn't high enough. He wanted to go bigger. So he and some friends built a 20-foot ramp with the goal to get some huge jumps with their bikes. He added a weedeater engine to his bike for extra power and was towed to the base of the ramp by a motorcycle for added speed. Talk about a daredevil move! The ramp was a success. Mat jumped the 20-foot ramp and went 20 feet higher into the air. This was the highest anyone had ever jumped. But while trying to get even bigger air, Mat crashed. He ruptured his spleen and nearly died. The doctors said if he had been twenty minutes later getting to the hospital, he wouldn't have made it.

While the crash slowed him down for a little while, there was still no stopping Mat. The X Games were just getting started and Mat was asked to help with making the experience better for BMX freestyle riders. He helped make sure the ramps were well designed. And of course, he competed there as well. He landed one of his many famous moves for the first time at The X Games. Early in his career, Mat had been the first person ever to land the 900, which is two and a half spins in the air while on a bike. At the 2002 X Games, Mat told his wife, Jaci, that he was going to try something special...something BIG. He asked her to sit in a certain spot where he would see her and their daughter right before he launched. Mat performed and landed the first-ever 900 with no hands!

Mat blazed the trail for BMX freestylers everywhere. Because of his desire for more height in his jumps, X Games management built the ramps still used today (known as Mega Ramp) which launched the Big Air competition. Mega Ramp is 73 feet tall and riders have to ride an elevator to the top! Riders launch off the ramp on their bikes and the dynamics allow them to perform incredible tricks and stunts. Of course, there is still risk involved. You probably shouldn't try this at home with your own Mega Ramp.

Even though your mom may not appreciate his daredevil behavior, Mat is a great role model. He was just a normal kid from a small town who made a big impact because he was able to dream big. He found what he was passionate about and he worked hard to achieve his goals. And perhaps most importantly, he was really happy doing it. So whether your goals include jumping off a bike ramp, or perhaps something a little less dangerous, work hard and stay passionate.

Tennis Star Nearly Loses His Legs on the Titanic

Getting to be on the first voyage of the Titanic would have seemed like quite the privilege, at least at the time. We all know how that story ends now though. But out of all the sorrowful tales that came out of that journey, this story is one of amazing triumph.

Richard Norris Williams was a promising young tennis player. His parents were American, but Richard was born in Sweden where he learned to play tennis at a young age. He was very good and won the Swiss Championship in 1911. His plans included returning to America where he would enroll at Harvard and play tennis.

Richard wasn't even supposed to be on the Titanic, as his trip had been planned for a few weeks prior. An unfortunate bout of the measles delayed his journey to America, which had him and his father boarding the Titanic on April 10th, 1912. I'm sure it seemed exciting to be involved in this historic occasion as a passenger on the beautiful ship's maiden voyage.

But when the Titanic struck the iceberg just four days after setting off, I would imagine the overall feeling from the passengers was one of panic and despair. Richard and his father left their stateroom to see what was happening. They passed a door where passengers were stuck inside their cabin, yelling for help. Richard used his shoulder to throw the door open, freeing the people trapped inside. For this, he was strongly reprimanded by a crew member of the ship who threatened to report him for causing damage to the ship. As if it wasn't sinking into the ocean!

The Titanic sank within three hours of hitting the iceberg. During this time, Richard and his father wandered around the ship and even visited the ship's exercise room where they rode stationary bikes to try and keep warm. Of course, we all know that nothing could be done to save the ship. As sinking became imminent, Richard and his father jumped into the icy water below. As they were swimming to find something to help them float, the ship sank the rest of the way. Unfortunately, one of the giant smoke tunnels fell where his father was swimming, which killed him. Richard had to swim for some distance before he came upon a collapsible boat. He swam alongside for a little time before he was able to pull himself into the lifeboat.

Even on the lifeboat, his lower legs were submerged in the frigid water. The small boat was rescued by the ship, the RMS Carpathia. Once on board, the ship's doctor on the Carpathia examined Richard's legs. He had suffered from severe frostbite and the doctor advised him to amputate them. Unwilling to sacrifice his tennis career, Richard told him, "I'm going to need those legs."

Richard set a plan in motion to restore circulation in his legs, walking the ship's deck every two hours for the remainder of the journey. The plan paid off. Within a few months, he was back on the tennis courts, this time playing in America.

Richard began to rack up championships, winning several years at the intercollegiate level and also winning the prestigious US Championships in 1914 and 1916. He took a brief break from the sport to serve as a soldier in World War I where he was awarded a Legion of Honor and the Croix de Guerre for his service.

After his military service, Richard went back to the tennis courts. He continued with his winning ways and in 1924 got a chance to compete in the Olympics. Even though he was playing on a sprained ankle, Richard and his partner managed to clinch the title in the mixed doubles, making them both Olympic gold medalists.

He retired from tennis at 44 years old and was inducted into the Tennis Hall of Fame in 1957. By taking charge of his health that fateful night on the rescue ship, Richard was able to continue to have a long and extremely successful tennis career, despite all of the tragedy that happened with the sinking of the Titanic. What could you achieve if you made it a point to be on top of your own health?

Love and Meatballs

You've probably thrown part of a sandwich to a stray dog before. It feels really good to feed an animal that is hungry. Mikael Lindnord was the kind of guy to do that as well. Mikael was eating with his three other Swedish teammates one day nearing the end of a 430-mile-long adventure race in Ecuador. This was serious stuff. Suddenly, there was this scruffy dog wagging his tail at the team. Mikael was eating canned meatballs and it was important that these athletes get plenty of protein to fill them up to finish the next two legs of the race. But he tossed a meatball (a Swedish meatball, of course) to the dirty little dog.

That was all this dog needed. He decided right there that Mikael was his new best friend. But this race wasn't just in Ecuador. It was in the Amazon rainforest during the Adventure Racing World Championship. This was not the place that anyone would expect to run into a stray dog. Yet, there he was.

Adventure racers are some of the best athletes in the world. This race had all the best in the sport participating. The year was 2014. 50 teams started the race. Not all of them would finish. Adventure racing is an extreme sport. It can be more about survival than racing. It involves technical rock climbing, kayaking, hiking, and cycling. But all of that is done in the harshest conditions possible. You have to be willing to

suffer. These races are brutal. Sometimes racers die! This is one serious (and dangerous) sport. Mikael's team was called Team Peak Performance, representing their home country of Sweden. Teams from all over the world were there. But Mikael's Swedish squad was one of the best. They had survived nearly four days of this race through the Amazon rainforest. They were only a couple of hours behind the leaders which meant they had a chance to win. They had made it to a transition area and were eating quickly. And there was this dirty jungle dog.

After he gratefully gobbled up the meatball, the team headed out. Their short rest was over. They had 20 miles of muddy rainforest to get through. They thought it was cute that the dog seemed to be tagging along with them. But none of the team expected that to last. The dog had probably never had a Swedish meatball before. It must have been the best thing he ever tasted! And dogs know when people are nice. The dog had a good feeling about this crew and he knew that he had found a new pack. It didn't matter that he had a wound on his back and was hurt. It didn't even matter that these weirdos were hiking through one of the harshest environments on earth. This dog was used to it.

When the team would stop to rest, they kept sharing their precious food. They could tell that the dog was exhausted so they gave him more than they ate themselves. The dog kept up for 20 muddy miles. The dog now had not just a new pack, but a new name as well. Mikael had named him Arthur, after King Arthur from the Knights of the Round Table tales of medieval England. They were now at the Cojimies River. This would be the last leg of the race. Mikael and the rest of the team felt that sadly, their time with Arthur was over. The race finished with a 36-mile kayaking paddle down the river that would take them 14 hours to complete. A kayak is not like a canoe, there's not a lot of room in there. You sit down inside them and there's really just room for your legs. Early the next morning, they would have to say goodbye.

The sun had not yet risen, but it was the final day of the race and time to get paddling. They said their goodbyes to Arthur and pushed off through the darkness into the river. But Arthur would NOT be left behind. He immediately jumped out into the river and was paddling as fast as his little paws could go to keep up. Mikael wasn't about to leave Arthur behind then. He grabbed the little dog and pulled him into his kayak. The people in the transition area cheered. Arthur was truly part of the team.

Mikael said about kayaking with Arthur, "It was not easy. He was shivering. We were also shivering, of course, but I had my Gore-tex jacket - so I put my Gore-tex jacket over him." Staffan (one of the team members) would later say, "It was so clear, he was a part of us...There was something bigger in taking care of this dog than winning." And it's a good thing because paddling with Arthur was definitely slower than paddling without him. Over the course of the day, the little guy kept jumping out of Mikael's kayak to chase fish. But the 4 person, 1 dog team would eventually cross the finish line. They finished 12th out of 50 teams. Not bad! But their odyssey was just getting started in a lot of ways.

The team would, of course, leave Ecuador and go back home to Sweden. After finishing the race with them, there's no way they were leaving their new teammate behind. This was tough although news of what had happened was starting to spread. Photos of Arthur adventuring with the team went viral. Arthur had become a sensation. He would need medical care to help heal the wounds he had gotten before teaming up with Mikael. Mikael thought that he had probably been mistreated by some people. Both the Ecuadorian and Swedish governments got involved to work something out. Eventually, Arthur was well enough to make the 6,500-mile trip to live with his new family. But it would be much easier riding in an airplane than trotting along through the rainforest! Things got much easier for Arthur in Sweden having joined Mikael's family. Lots of food with a soft bed...life was now really, really good for the cute little jungle dog who bonded with Mikael over a meatball. Mikael still takes Arthur out for hiking adventures though and would say about his rainforest race experience with Arthur, "It's the single best thing I've ever done."

Ukrainian Heavyweight Champions Now Fighting Against a Real Invasion

When you think of boxing brothers, you have to think of the Klitschko brothers, Vitali and Wladimir. Together, they dominated heavyweight boxing for more than a decade. Combined, they have won a staggering total of 40 heavyweight title fights. That's simply incredible. They've won 109 fights and only lost 7 times. 94 of those wins were knockouts. And here's something fascinating. Older brother, Vitali, was NEVER knocked down. It's pretty impressive to never be knocked out, but never even knocked down? Most boxers get knocked down, but not Vitali. Vitali stands at a massive 6 foot 7 inches with Wladimir being just an inch shorter. They fill up any doorway that they walk through. The two are very close. Over the course of their careers, nearly every time one of them fights, the other is literally in their corner to help with water and bandaging cuts. Vitali liked to say, "Our opponents don't know our secret weapon. Even with only one person in the ring, they're fighting two people." Their story is truly a spectacular one.

During their dominant run, they were often offered massive amounts of money to fight each other. But their mom made them promise that they would never fight each other. Wladimir said, "I wouldn't do it, even for $1 billion. You can't put a price on your mother's heart." They are Ukrainian. When they were growing up, Ukraine was part of the Soviet Union. Now it is an independent country. Their father was a colonel in the Soviet air force. He was one of the first soldiers on the scene to clean up the Chernobyl nuclear disaster. This was a nuclear plant that exploded and became a very dangerous situation. The Klitschko family lived just 60 miles away. Everyone had to be evacuated and most of the soldiers who responded died from nuclear poisoning. The boys' dad survived but cancer that was caused by his working there eventually killed him. The brothers were lucky. The army brought back the helicopters and vehicles used at Chernobyl to the town where the Klitschko family lived to be washed. The water that came off of those vehicles was radioactive. Wladimir played in that water by floating paper boats on it.

Vitali is 5 years older than Wladimir and wasn't a traditional boxer, to begin with. He loved karate and racked up a 34-2 record as a kickboxer. Vitali then became a boxer and started off his career with 25 straight knockouts of his opponents. He was born to fight and he loved it. Wladimir wasn't as passionate about fighting as his older brother. Maybe that's because he was introduced to it by having his older brother punch him once with a boxing glove on. Wladimir says his brother hit him so hard that he saw stars! But Wladimir was so strong and big that he started boxing as well and eventually grew to love it. Before he turned professional, Wladimir won a gold medal at the Olympics for Ukraine. Vitali was a great champion who finished his career with a record of 45-2 with 41 knockouts. His only two losses were because of injury. And did I mention that he was never knocked down, even once? Wladimir wasn't quite as unbeatable as his brother but had an amazing career as well. He finished 64-5 with 53 knockouts. Not too shabby!

What's really interesting is what the brothers have done since retiring from the ring. Both brothers got educated and got PhDs which means they are considered doctors. They are sometimes jokingly referred to as Dr. Ironfist and Dr. Steelhammer. Vitali got into politics when he retired. He first became an advisor to the President that he campaigned for and helped get elected. Vitali was then elected to the Kyiv City Council. Kyiv is Ukraine's capital city. Eventually, he was elected mayor and is still the Mayor of Kyiv to this day. He has been reelected several times and even started his own political party, the Ukrainian Democratic Alliance for Reform. Vitali has been dedicated to stamping out corruption in government and has had a very successful political career. Wladimir, since retiring, has been an adjunct professor in Switzerland teaching college students. He also runs a boxing promotion company.

Now, the two brothers, two of the most successful heavyweight fighters of all time, find themselves in the middle of a new fight. In 2022, Ukraine was invaded by Russia. Both brothers have sworn that they will not leave and that they will fight for their country's independence. The Russian president, Vladimir Putin, does not like the Klitschko brothers at all. They might be the most famous and influential Ukrainians of all time. Both brothers have always been each other's biggest supporter. Wladimir wasn't about to let Vitali face the Russian threat alone. He has joined the Ukrainian Defense Force and has been on the front lines of the fight for Ukraine. Even though both brothers are millionaires and could afford to live anywhere in the world, they want to stay and defend their country. Wladimir has done lots of interviews to bring attention to what the Ukrainians are dealing with as they fight. He says "There is no army, no weapon that can break the spirit and the will of the Ukrainian people. This is our land. This is our home." Vitali adds, "We're not interested in how strong the Russian army is, we're ready to fight. And we're ready to die for our home country and for our families because it's our home. It's our future and somebody wants to come to our home and steal our future from us."

The ending to this story is still unwritten. As I am writing this, the Klitschko brothers are with their people fighting against the Russian army that has invaded their country. I hope for peace. I hope for an end to the fighting. The bravery of the Ukrainian people has been inspiring. War is a terrible thing. It's much more serious than boxing, but the Ukrainian people are certainly as tough as anyone. You know that by how tough Vitali and Wladimir have been their entire lives. I sure wouldn't want to fight them. Hopefully, this part of the world will have peace again soon. But no matter what happens, Vitali and Wladimir Klitschko will bravely face it, side by side...just as they've always faced everything.

YOUR REVIEW

What if I told you that just one minute out of your life could bring joy and jubilation to everyone working at a kids book company?

What am I yapping about? I'm talking about leaving this book a review.

I promise you, we take them **VERY seriously**. Don't believe me?

Each time right after someone just like you leaves this book a review, a little siren goes off right here in our office. And when it does we all pump our fists with pure happiness.

A disco ball pops out of the ceiling, flashing lights come on...it's party time!

Roger, our marketing guy, always and I mean always, starts flossing like a crazy person and keeps it up for awhile. He's pretty good at it. (It's a silly dance he does, not cleaning his teeth)

Sarah, our office manager, runs outside and gives everyone up and down the street high fives. She's always out of breath when she comes back but it's worth it!

Our editors work up in the loft and when they hear the review siren, they all jump into the swirly slide and ride down into a giant pit of marshmallows where they roll around and make marshmallow angels. (It's a little weird, but tons of fun)

So reviews are a pretty big deal for us.

It means a lot and helps others just like you who also might enjoy this book, find it too.

You're the best!
From all of us goofballs at Big Dreams Kids Books

Made in United States
North Haven, CT
28 September 2022